THE COMPLETE GUIDE TO PARENTING YOUR CHILD WITH ADHD

PROVEN STRESS-FREE SOLUTIONS TO BUILD CONFIDENCE, CONNECTION, AND CONSISTENCY AT HOME AND SCHOOL

DR. VICTORIA BARCLAY-TIMMIS

© **Copyright Dr Victoria Barclay-Timmis, 2025 - All rights reserved.**

The content within this book may not be reproduced, duplicated or transmitted without direct written permission from the author or the publisher.

Under no circumstances will any blame or legal responsibility be held against the publisher, or author, for any damages, reparation, or monetary loss due to the information contained within this book. Either directly or indirectly. You are responsible for your own choices, actions, and results.

Legal Notice:

This book is copyright protected. This book is only for personal use. You cannot amend, distribute, sell, use, quote or paraphrase any part, of the content within this book, without the consent of the author or publisher.

Disclaimer Notice:

Please note the information contained within this document is for educational and entertainment purposes only. All effort has been expended to present accurate, up-to-date, and reliable, complete information. No warranties of any kind are declared or implied. Readers acknowledge that the author is not engaging in the rendering of legal, financial, medical or professional advice. The content within this book has been derived from various sources. Please consult a licensed professional before attempting any techniques outlined in this book.

By reading this document, the reader agrees that under no circumstances is the author responsible for any losses, direct or indirect, which are incurred as a result of the use of the information contained within this document, including, but not limited to, — errors, omissions, or inaccuracies.

CONTENTS

Introduction	5
1. Understanding ADHD	9
2. Building Empathy and Connection	35
3. Navigating Daily Challenges with Confidence and Calm	49
4. Emotional Regulation and Well-being	67
5. Cost-effective Resources and Strategies	89
6. Navigating the Education System	99
7. Community and Support Networks	119
8. Planning for the Future	129
Conclusion and Takeaways	151

BONUS CONTENT

ADHD Assessment – What to Expect	157
Explaining ADHD to Your Child, Step-by-Step	165
Exploring Effective, Evidence-Based Therapy Options for Children with ADHD	171
A Fun, Family-Focused Mindfulness and Self-Compassion Curriculum	185
Author Biography	197
Bibliography and Reference List	199

INTRODUCTION

The morning sun streams through the blinds, bathing the kitchen in a warm glow. Yet, despite the golden light, the scene before you feels anything but serene. Your child, a whirlwind of energy, zips from room to room, cereal spilling, one shoe missing, and joyfully oblivious to the chaos left in their wake. You, gripping your second cup of coffee, glance at the clock. The day hasn't officially begun, but you already feel the weight of the hours ahead pressing down on you. At this moment, you might wonder: *Is it possible to find calm in this chaos?*

If this sounds familiar, you're in good company. Parenting a child with ADHD can often feel as challenging juggling flaming torches while riding a rollercoaster—unpredictable, intense, and requiring constant adjustment, yet also filled with moments of awe, joy, and deep connection when you find your rhythm. This book is here to provide a guide to maximize the positive moments; it is filled with empathy, understanding, and actionable strategies to help you and your child not just survive but thrive.

Let me introduce myself. My name is Victoria, and I am a clinical psychologist with 12 years of experience in private practice. My professional life has been devoted to helping individuals and families navigate the complexities of life through evidence-based strategies. I've also lectured and supervised university students, developed and delivered group therapy programs, and conducted PhD research on self-compassion, mindfulness, resilience, and well-being for parents and children. But beyond my credentials, I'm a mother and the wife of an educator, and I've lived and breathed the realities of balancing family life with the unique challenges ADHD brings.

I know firsthand that ADHD is often misunderstood. Perhaps someone has told you your child needs more discipline or that they'll grow out of their difficulties. These misconceptions can make you feel isolated and disheartened. But let me assure you: ADHD is not the result of bad parenting, nor is it a phase. It's a unique way of experiencing the world, and with the right tools and mindset, you can help your child harness their strengths and overcome their challenges.

This book isn't just focused on your child; it offers strategies for you, too. Parenting is an ever-evolving journey. There will be days when you feel like you've got it all together and others when it feels like everything is falling apart. And that's okay. There's no such thing as a perfect parent. What matters is showing up—failing, learning, and trying again. Treat yourself with the same compassion you extend to your child. You're growing alongside them.

Throughout these pages, you'll find practical guidance to help you address daily struggles, from morning routines to bedtime battles. We'll debunk common myths about ADHD, and I'll share ways to build empathy, confidence, and connection in your home. You'll also learn how to advocate for your child in the education system, foster their emotional regulation, and find cost-effective resources that make a real difference. As we look to the future, I'll guide you in preparing your child for the transition to adulthood, equipping them with independence and self-advocacy skills. To illustrate I will also share with you some stories from the families I have worked with directly (all names and identifying information have been changed, of course!)

Parenting a child with ADHD is challenging, yes, but it's also filled with opportunities to grow together. Community is a key part of this journey. This book will show you how to build a support network, connect with others who understand your experience, and discover the comfort of shared stories.

Together, we'll forge a brighter path. Along the way, you'll gain valuable tools, practical strategies, and, most importantly, renewed hope. You'll see your child's confidence grow and your family's bond strengthen. While the road may have its challenges, the rewards will be deeply fulfilling. So, let's take this step forward together. Your child's story is still unfolding, and this adventure is just beginning.

ONE
UNDERSTANDING ADHD

Your child stands in front of a mountain of school papers spilled across the kitchen table, each one crumpled and stained with snack smudges. You watch them struggle, caught between wanting to help and trying to let them figure it out. Your heart aches as you see the frustration build in their eyes. Why can't they just sit still and focus? Why is every day a new challenge? Parenting a child with ADHD can feel like a never-ending cycle of questions and uncertainties, with each day presenting its own unique set of trials. You may question everything in these moments, from your parenting skills to your child's future. This chapter explores the neurological underpinnings, behavioral patterns, and societal misconceptions about ADHD, helping you understand the condition while recognizing your child's unique potential and challenges.

DEBUNKING COMMON ADHD MYTHS

The belief that ADHD stems from "bad" parenting is one of the most persistent and damaging myths. It burdens parents unnecessarily, making them feel their children's behaviors directly result from their own failings, when in fact, ADHD is a complex condition rooted in the brain's biology. It's not about parenting styles or discipline; it's about understanding how your child's brain works differently and discovering strategies to support their unique needs.

Another pervasive myth is that children with ADHD are lazy or unmotivated. You've likely heard this from well-meaning relatives or teachers, and it's frustrating. The reality is that ADHD can make it difficult for children to regulate their attention and energy, which can be misunderstood as laziness. Yet, these children often display incredible focus, or "hyperfocus," on tasks that truly engage them. They can be incredibly passionate and motivated when they find something that captures their interest and ignites their curiosity and drive.

This misunderstanding of motivation is closely related to another common myth: that all individuals with ADHD are hyperactive. While some children exhibit high energy levels, others might seem dreamy or inattentive without the hyperactivity. According to the DSM-5 (a manual published by the American Psychiatric Association that lists and describes criteria for diagnosing mental disorders), ADHD presents in three types: predominantly inattentive, predominantly hyperactive-impulsive, and combined.

- **Predominantly inattentive** type is characterized by difficulty sustaining attention, frequent daydreaming, being easily distracted, forgetfulness, and struggles with organization or following through on tasks. This is the most common type, accounting for approximately 30–40% of ADHD diagnoses. It tends to be more frequently identified in girls and often goes underdiagnosed due to less disruptive behaviors compared to the hyperactive-impulsive type.
- **Predominantly hyperactive-impulsive** type involves constant fidgeting, an inability to stay seated, excessive talking, interrupting others, and acting without thinking, often leading to impulsive decisions or risky behaviors. This type is less common, representing about 10–15% of ADHD diagnoses. It is more frequently diagnosed in younger children, as hyperactive and impulsive

behaviors tend to be more noticeable in early childhood.
- **Combined type** is characterized by a mixture of symptoms from both the inattentive and hyperactive-impulsive types, including challenges with focus and organization alongside high energy levels, impulsivity, and difficulty regulating behaviors. Combined type is the most diagnosed subtype of ADHD, making up approximately 50–60% of cases. It is the type most seen in clinical settings because it includes a mix of both inattentive and hyperactive-impulsive symptoms, which are often more disruptive and noticeable.

Understanding this diversity in how ADHD symptoms might present can help you better identify your child's needs and tailor your approach accordingly.

It's also a common misconception that ADHD only affects children. While the brain's prefrontal cortex continues to mature into the mid-20s, leading to natural reductions in some ADHD symptoms, others often persist in adolescence and adulthood. However, environmental factors, such as decreased academic pressures, structured work settings, and supportive relationships, can make symptoms less disruptive. Additionally, many individuals with ADHD develop effective coping strategies through therapy, medication, or personal experience. Recognizing the potential for ADHD to continue beyond childhood is crucial for preparing to provide long-term support, ensuring that individuals can lead successful, fulfilling lives regardless of their diagnosis.

Finally, while some may misinterpret an ADHD diagnosis as a negative label or stigma that follows your child, many successful figures, from athletes to artists, have ADHD and attribute their success to their unique ways of thinking. For example, Michael Phelps, the most decorated Olympian in history, and actor Jim Carrey credit ADHD for fueling their drive and creativity. An ADHD diagnosis doesn't define your child; it simply provides a framework to understand their behavior and needs. Personally, I like to think of ADHD as a superpower that can endow individuals with distinctive strengths, such as heightened creativity, passion, and resilience. By recognizing and nurturing these attributes, your child can learn to harness their 'superpower' to thrive and excel in their endeavors.

THE (BASIC) NEUROSCIENCE OF ADHD: WHAT EVERY PARENT SHOULD KNOW

Picture your child's brain as a bustling city, where the prefrontal cortex acts as the traffic controller, working to keep everything running smoothly. This part of the brain, located just behind the forehead, is responsible for executive functions like decision-making, impulse control, and attention management. In children with ADHD, the prefrontal cortex sometimes struggles to coordinate with other parts of the brain, causing traffic jams and detours that lead to impulsivity and distraction.

Meanwhile, the limbic system, the brain's emotional center, can respond with heightened sensitivity, like a sudden storm rolling in on a sunny day—unexpected, intense, and sometimes overwhelming.

Now, imagine the brain's neurotransmitters, dopamine and norepinephrine, as delivery trucks zipping through the city, carrying vital supplies that help regulate attention and motivation. In ADHD, these trucks may be delayed, understocked, or rerouted, leading to bottlenecks and missed deliveries that disrupt efficient thinking and focus. It's as if some traffic lights are stuck on red while others flash erratically, making the city's highways unpredictable and chaotic.

The basal ganglia, another key structure, functions like the city's subway system, responsible for facilitating smooth transitions from thought to action. When this system falters, your child might miss their stop, struggling to complete tasks or shift from one activity to another. Similarly, the reticular activating system, the brain's alertness regulator, can behave like an overzealous subway alarm—sometimes buzzing relentlessly, causing hyperactivity, or remaining silent, leading to inattentiveness and daydreaming.

Finally, the amygdala, which governs emotional responses, acts as the brain's fire alarm. In children with ADHD, it can be hypersensitive, sometimes misinterpreting minor setbacks as full-blown crises. This is why something as small as a misplaced pencil can feel like an emergency, triggering an outsized emotional response.

FROM UNDERSTANDING TO EMPATHY AND TAILORED TREATMENT

Recognizing these neurological differences and how they impact your child's daily experiences is essential for developing empathy. For instance, understanding that impulsivity stems from disrupted communication between brain regions helps you reframe outbursts not as intentional defiance but as the brain's struggle to self-regulate. Similarly, grasping the role of neurotransmitter imbalances equips you to consider interventions like medication or behavioral therapy as tools to balance this intricate system.

Think of managing ADHD as maintaining a complex ecosystem. Reducing noise pollution in the "city"—by creating a structured, calm environment—can help your child's brain function more smoothly. Encouraging regular "exercise routes" for the brain through physical activity boosts dopamine, ensuring the brain functions optimally, like greasing the gears of a well-oiled machine. Visual aids act as clear road signs, guiding your child through tasks and preventing mental traffic jams.

Ongoing research provides hope, shedding light on ADHD's intricacies and offering new management strategies. Innovations in neuroimaging technology reveal the brain's activity in real time, akin to viewing a live traffic map. This technology helps identify specific patterns or disruptions in the brain's functioning, allowing for more tailored interventions. Therapies like neurofeedback teach children to regulate their brain activity, like learning to operate a complex control tower. Children are provided with real-time feedback on how their brain is functioning, and they are rewarded for producing specific brainwave patterns that correspond to desired mental states, such as calmness, focus, or emotional regulation.

Connecting the dots between the brain's structures and behaviors gives you a roadmap to support your child better. ADHD isn't a broken system; it's a unique cityscape filled with potential—a place where, with the right tools and understanding, your child can navigate their challenges and thrive.

While these neurological differences can feel overwhelming, understanding them equips you with the knowledge to support your child better. Recognizing triggers, such as a noisy environment or lack of sleep, can help you anticipate and mitigate potential meltdowns. Tailoring your parenting approach means embracing flexibility, such as using visual aids or setting clear, concise instructions to guide your child through daily tasks. Research-backed therapies, like neurofeedback or mindfulness practices, can also help manage symptoms effectively, giving you more tools to support your child. These therapies (and more) will be discussed in more detail in a later chapter.

RECOGNIZING ADHD SYMPTOMS AND BEHAVIORS

Your child is at the dinner table, fork in hand, lost in the intricate patterns of the tablecloth while their meal goes cold. You call their name once, twice, three times, and still, their attention drifts like a kite on a windy day. This inattentiveness is a hallmark of ADHD, manifesting as distractibility that can turn simple tasks into Herculean efforts. Some children may struggle with staying organized, their backpacks a jumble of papers and pens, while others might face emotional dysregulation, where feelings erupt like a geyser, unexpected and intense.

ADHD often manifests in behaviors that can easily be overlooked or misunderstood. For example, a child might frequently daydream during lessons, which can be mistaken for a lack of interest. Others might exhibit subtle signs of impulsivity, like blurting out answers before a question is finished or interrupting conversations—behaviors that could be seen as rudeness rather than symptoms of ADHD. Additionally, children with ADHD might avoid tasks requiring sustained mental effort, not out of defiance but because such tasks can feel insurmountable to them.

Other subtle signs include losing personal items like toys, homework, or jackets more often than peers. This forgetfulness is not carelessness but rather an indication of challenges with working memory. A child might also seem overly emotional, with reactions that appear exaggerated for the situation, such as intense frustration over a minor setback.

Social challenges can also be a clue. Children with ADHD may struggle to pick up on social cues, leading to misunderstandings with peers. They might appear overly eager to join a group but fail to recognize when their behavior is intrusive, which can impact friendships. Similarly, time management difficulties, often called "time blindness," can make them late or cause them to underestimate how long tasks will take.

Navigating ADHD symptoms requires a detective's eye. Keeping a behavior diary can help you identify patterns—what happens before, during, and after episodes of inattention or impulsivity? Environmental factors, like noise levels or hunger, often play a role in these behaviors. Collaborating with teachers or caregivers can provide additional insights, creating a fuller picture to guide interventions.

Understanding these symptoms isn't about labelling your child but equipping yourself with tools to help them thrive.

Recognizing the overlap of ADHD with conditions like anxiety or autism can also ensure an accurate diagnosis, paving the way for effective strategies tailored to your child's needs.

DID YOU KNOW? TEN LITTLE-KNOWN ADHD FACTS

1. ADHD is one of the most studied psychiatric disorders, with thousands of research studies conducted over the past few decades.
2. People with ADHD often excel in creative and dynamic environments where they can leverage their out-of-the-box thinking.
3. ADHD affects boys and girls differently, with girls more likely to be underdiagnosed due to quieter symptoms like daydreaming.
4. The condition is highly heritable, with genetics accounting for about 75% of ADHD cases.
5. Adults with ADHD are at a higher risk for certain health conditions, such as obesity and sleep disorders, due to challenges with impulse control and routines.
6. Many historical figures, including Thomas Edison and Mozart, displayed traits consistent with ADHD.
7. Physical exercise can significantly reduce ADHD symptoms by boosting dopamine levels in the brain.
8. Time blindness, or difficulty sensing the passage of time, is a common but less well-known symptom of ADHD.
9. ADHD can coexist with many other conditions, such

as anxiety, depression, or learning disabilities; this is known as comorbidity.
10. While often seen as a disorder, ADHD can be reframed as a different way of thinking, with many individuals excelling in fast-paced or high-energy professions.

ADHD AND NEURODIVERSITY: EMBRACING DIFFERENCES

Neurodiversity celebrates the unique and varied ways our brains work. Within this spectrum, ADHD shines as a source of creativity, energy, and innovative thinking. Embracing neurodiversity means moving beyond stereotypes and recognizing your child's unique traits as strengths waiting to be nurtured.

ADHD often gifts individuals with abundant creativity. For example, Leonardo da Vinci, the Renaissance genius, displayed traits consistent with ADHD: intense curiosity and unfinished projects. Similarly, studies suggest that children with ADHD excel at divergent thinking. Divergent thinking is the ability to generate multiple unique solutions to open-ended problems, a key component of creativity. A review published by CHADD (Children and Adults with Attention-Deficit/Hyperactivity Disorder) examined 31 studies on ADHD and creativity. The findings indicated that in children, higher levels of ADHD symptoms were associated with increased divergent thinking abilities. This suggests that children with ADHD can thrive in environments that value innovation and flexibility.

Children with ADHD may also demonstrate remarkable empathy and emotional sensitivity. Although they might struggle with emotional regulation, their ability to connect deeply with others often makes them excellent listeners and loyal friends. For instance, they might notice when a peer feels down and offer comfort in ways others overlook. Embracing these qualities means acknowledging the emotional intelligence that can shine through ADHD's challenges.

ADHD can also enhance adaptability. Children with ADHD often learn to think on their feet because their brains are wired for fast-paced environments. Consider a child who thrives during chaotic group activities or excels in brainstorming sessions that demand quick thinking. This adaptability is a powerful asset in dynamic situations, such as sports or creative performances, where rapid decision-making is key.

Practical ways to harness these strengths include allowing your child to explore their passions and interests freely. If they love art, encourage them to draw or paint without worrying about staying within the lines. If they're fascinated by space, provide books, videos, or even star charts to feed their curiosity. This engagement channels their energy and builds confidence in their unique abilities.

Fostering acceptance in your home and community creates an environment where your child can thrive. Small adjustments, like visual schedules or creating quiet spaces for focused tasks, can turn potential obstacles into stepping-stones. For example, a homework station equipped with a timer and noise-canceling headphones can transform the struggle of staying on task into an achievable challenge. You will find many more suggestions and strategies in the later chapters of this book.

Sharing stories of neurodiverse individuals and connecting with advocacy groups can also provide comfort and inspiration, reminding you that your family is not alone. For instance, organizations like the ADHD Foundation offer resources and success stories highlighting how ADHD traits have contributed to achievements in fields like entrepreneurship, entertainment, and science. Knowing others have faced similar challenges and thrived can offer hope and direction. (More on this topic later!)

By shifting the focus from what a child with ADHD "lacks" to what they possess in abundance, you can help them see themselves not as a problem to be fixed but as a person with gifts waiting to be nurtured. This perspective changes how you see your child and helps them see themselves with pride and possibility. As low self-esteem is more prevalent in children with ADHD, it is essential that parents change the narrative from one of struggle and frustration to one of strengths, growth, and potential.

THE IMPACT OF ADHD ON FAMILY DYNAMICS

ADHD doesn't just affect your child—it influences the entire family. Sibling rivalry can intensify when one child seems to demand more attention. In some cases, a sibling with ADHD might feel overlooked or frustrated by the extra time and energy devoted to their brother or sister. They might question why their sibling seems to receive special treatment. For instance, during family game night, your child with ADHD might struggle to take turns or follow the rules, sparking arguments or feelings of unfairness among siblings. These moments can accumulate, creating tension that requires careful navigation.

Meanwhile, stress can strain your relationship with your partner as you navigate daily challenges. You may find yourselves taking on distinct roles: one parent becomes the enforcer while the other becomes the nurturer, leading to disagreements about discipline and approach. For example, one parent might feel exasperated when a carefully crafted plan goes awry due to an impulsive outburst, while the other focuses on mitigating the emotional aftermath.

Parenting a child with ADHD can also create logistical challenges that ripple through family life. Unexpected school calls or last-minute project crises can derail carefully planned schedules, leaving everyone scrambling. Family outings may require additional preparation to account for potential triggers, such as loud noises or crowded spaces, which can turn what should be relaxing experiences into sources of stress.

Building open communication is key to managing these dynamics. Family meetings allow everyone to voice their feelings and celebrate successes. For example, siblings might appreciate a chance to express their frustrations and have their concerns acknowledged. These meetings also provide an opportunity to set clear expectations and discuss strategies for handling conflicts constructively.

Siblings, too, need time and understanding. Carving out regular, one-on-one time with each child reassures them of their importance. It can be as simple as a shared bedtime story or a solo trip to their favorite park. This dedicated time helps balance the scales and strengthens relationships.

Educating siblings about ADHD in age-appropriate ways can transform frustration into empathy; for example, explaining that their brother or sister's impulsiveness isn't intentional but a result of how their brain works can foster greater compassion. This understanding can help siblings shift from seeing themselves as competitors for parental attention to allies in their sibling's journey.

External support systems, such as friends or community groups, provide much-needed relief. Leaning on others reminds you that you don't have to face these challenges alone. Grandparents who can help with childcare, friends who can listen without judgment, or support groups where you can share experiences all play critical roles in lightening the load.

Another impactful strategy is involving the whole family in solutions. For instance, creating a shared calendar can help everyone stay organized and reduce stress around schedules. Assigning small responsibilities to each family member fosters teamwork and a sense of shared purpose, helping everyone feel included and valued.

Navigating family dynamics with ADHD is undeniably challenging, but it's also an opportunity to strengthen bonds and build resilience. By ensuring there is open communication, setting clear expectations, and involving siblings in the conversation, you create an environment where everyone feels seen and supported. The path may not always be smooth, but with more understanding and empathy, your family can thrive together, embracing each member's strengths and challenges.

ADHD THROUGH THE AGES: FROM CHILDHOOD TO ADOLESCENCE

As your child grows, the landscape of ADHD evolves, bringing unique challenges and opportunities at every stage. Understanding how ADHD traits manifest over time can help you tailor your parenting approach to meet their changing needs.

Early Childhood

In preschool, ADHD traits may present as boundless energy and curiosity. Your child might run laps around the playground while others sit quietly during story time. They may struggle with waiting their turn or keeping their hands to themselves, which could be misconstrued as defiance or poor manners. These behaviors often stem from impulsivity and an innate drive to explore.

Another hallmark of this stage is difficulty following instructions. A simple request like "Put on your shoes" might result in your child running off to find a toy or starting an unrelated activity. This isn't stubbornness; it's their brain struggling to prioritize and stay focused on a task.

Early School Years

As children enter primary school, academic demands can highlight ADHD-related challenges. A child with ADHD might fidget incessantly in their chair, tap their pencil on the desk, or blurt out answers in class, drawing the teacher's attention—not always in a positive way. At home, homework time might become a marathon of distractions, with every noise or object becoming a potential detour from the task.

Socially, they may struggle to make or keep friends. For example, they might dominate play by dictating the rules of a game or become overly emotional when things don't go their way. While these behaviors can lead to misunderstandings, they also reflect their desire to connect and strong emotions.

Middle Childhood

Late elementary school often brings organizational difficulties to the forefront. Your child might forget to bring home assignments, repeatedly lose their lunchbox, or find their schoolbag in constant chaos. Teachers may notice inconsistent performance—excelling in one subject one day and falling behind the next—leading to frustration for everyone involved.

Emotionally, this stage might bring heightened sensitivity to criticism. A simple comment like "You need to try harder" could trigger tears or withdrawal. Conversely, their curiosity and creativity might shine through in hands-on projects or imaginative storytelling.

Adolescence

Adolescence ushers in a whole new set of challenges. Hyperactivity may evolve into an inner restlessness, with your teenager tapping their foot, doodling on their notebook, or struggling to sit through long classes. Impulsivity might manifest as risk-taking behaviors, such as experimenting with dangerous activities or speaking out inappropriately during social interactions.

Academic pressures increase, as do the organizational demands of juggling multiple subjects, extracurricular activities, and social obligations. A missed deadline might spiral into feelings of inadequacy, especially as teens become more aware of their differences from peers.

Navigating friendships and romantic relationships can be challenging socially. For instance, a teen with ADHD might interrupt conversations without realizing it, leading to misunderstandings. However, their loyalty and enthusiasm often make them cherished friends once these hurdles are overcome.

Puberty adds another layer of complexity, as hormonal changes can amplify ADHD symptoms. Increased mood swings, difficulty regulating emotions, and heightened sensitivity are common. This is a time when patience and understanding from parents are crucial, as teens may feel overwhelmed by both internal and external changes. See Chapter 8 for more on the topic of supporting your child through adolescence.

Parenting through these transitions requires adaptability, open communication, and a willingness to learn alongside your child. The following Chapters of this book contain tools and strategies to enable you and your child to navigate the complexities of ADHD at every age, strengthening your relationship, and creating a foundation for lifelong success.

UNDERSTANDING THE INTERPLAY BETWEEN ADHD AND OTHER MENTAL HEALTH CONDITIONS

ADHD often coexists with other mental health conditions, creating a complex web of challenges that can significantly impact daily life. This phenomenon, known as comorbidity, highlights the need for a holistic approach to diagnosis and treatment. Here, we explore the interactions between ADHD and anxiety, depression, eating disorders, conduct disorders, obsessive-compulsive disorder (OCD), and tic disorders, incorporating prevalence rates to underline the scope of these overlaps.

ADHD and Anxiety

- Prevalence: Approximately 18% of children with ADHD also have an anxiety disorder, compared to 2% of children without ADHD (CHADD).
- Interplay: ADHD's challenges with organization, task completion, and social skills often lead to stressful situations that can trigger anxiety. Conversely, anxiety can exacerbate ADHD symptoms like distractibility and procrastination, creating a cycle of avoidance and heightened worry.
- Management Strategy: Cognitive-behavioral therapy (CBT) and mindfulness practices are particularly effective in managing these overlapping conditions.

ADHD and Depression

- Prevalence: Around 15% of children with ADHD experience depression, compared to 1% of children without ADHD (CHADD).
- Interplay: Chronic struggles with ADHD, such as repeated failures or social difficulties, can erode self-esteem and trigger depression. In turn, depression's fatigue and mental fog can intensify ADHD-related inattention and impulsivity.
- Management Strategy: Early intervention, CBT, and medication management are key to addressing both conditions effectively.

ADHD and Eating Disorders

- Prevalence: Individuals with ADHD are three times more likely to be diagnosed with an eating disorder (ADHD Foundation).
- Interplay: Impulsivity associated with ADHD can lead to binge eating, while difficulties with self-monitoring may result in neglecting nutritional needs. Emotional dysregulation often drives unhealthy eating habits as a coping mechanism.
- Management Strategy: A combination of therapy, nutritional guidance, and structured routines can help manage these behaviors.

ADHD and Conduct Disorders

- Prevalence: Conduct disorders occur in 27% of children with ADHD, compared to 2% without ADHD (CHADD).
- Interplay: Impulsivity and difficulty with emotional regulation can lead to aggressive or defiant behaviors. Challenges with authority figures and adherence to rules further exacerbate these issues.
- Management Strategy: Behavioural therapy and early intervention are critical in mitigating the risk of escalating behavioral challenges.

ADHD, OCD, and Tic Disorders

- Prevalence: Up to 30% of individuals with OCD also have ADHD (International OCD Foundation). Tic disorders, including Tourette syndrome, frequently overlap with ADHD.
- Interplay: The impulsivity of ADHD can intensify tic behaviors and create additional stress, while OCD's intrusive thoughts and compulsive behaviors add to the complexity of managing routines.
- Management Strategy: A tailored combination of therapy, medication, and structured support can effectively address these overlapping conditions.

Recognizing the prevalence and interplay of these comorbid conditions with ADHD underscores the importance of comprehensive assessment and individualized treatment plans. A holistic approach, integrating medication, therapy, and environmental adjustments, can significantly improve outcomes for individuals navigating these complex challenges.

INSIGHTS FROM THE THERAPY ROOM

As a clinical psychologist, I've spent many years working closely with children with ADHD and their families. One interaction stands out to me. A young boy—let's call him Liam—was referred to me because his parents were at their wit's end. Liam struggled in school, constantly being reprimanded for "acting out," his parents were exhausted from managing his outbursts and inattentiveness.

When I first met Liam, he was a bundle of nervous energy, fidgeting with the zipper of his jacket and avoiding eye contact. His parents informed me that Liam had been diagnosed with ADHD by his pediatrician, but they did not understand the condition or how to support their son. They were visibly stressed, anxious to find answers, but unsure where to start. I began by explaining ADHD in terms Liam could understand. I told him, "Your brain is like a race car with a super-powerful engine. It goes really fast, which is awesome for some things, like coming up with creative ideas. But sometimes, it needs better brakes to slow down. That's what we can work on together." His eyes lit up, and for the first time, he seemed to relax.

For his parents, I used a slightly different metaphor they could relate to. I described Liam's brain as a busy airport, with planes (thoughts) trying to take off and land simultaneously. "Sometimes, the control tower—the part of the brain that organizes everything—gets overwhelmed. That's why Liam might forget instructions or act impulsively." I saw a visible shift in their understanding by breaking down neuroscience into relatable terms: they quickly moved from frustration to empathy.

Throughout our sessions, it became obvious that Liam's self-esteem had suffered because of constantly finding himself in trouble, so we worked on fostering Liam's self-compassion. I taught him to recognize his strengths—his vivid imagination and quick thinking—and to give himself grace during challenging moments. "Everyone has things they're working on," I reminded him. Self-compassion became a cornerstone of his resilience, helping him bounce back from setbacks with greater confidence.

For his parents, we developed practical strategies, like visual schedules and setting achievable goals, to support Liam's daily routines. Perhaps most importantly, they adjusted their expectations and learned the value of modeling self-compassion. By showing Liam that mistakes were opportunities to learn rather than failures, they created a home environment where he felt safe to grow and thrive.

This experience, like many others, reaffirmed for me the importance of translating complex psychological concepts into accessible, actionable tools. When families understand ADHD in a way that fosters empathy and self-compassion, they unlock their ability to build resilience and nurture their child's potential. These moments of connection and growth remind me why I do this work and reinforce my belief that every child, regardless of their challenges, can flourish with the proper support.

CHAPTER REFLECTION

Understanding ADHD is not about fixing what's broken; it's about embracing and nurturing the unique ways your child experiences the world. As we've explored, ADHD is a complex interplay of neurological, behavioral, and emotional factors, often misunderstood yet brimming with opportunities for growth and connection. By debunking myths, delving into neuroscience, and recognizing symptoms with compassion, you equip yourself with the knowledge to meet your child where they are. ADHD may bring its challenges, but it also brings creativity, energy, and boundless potential. With understanding, patience, and a willingness to adapt, you can create a supportive environment where your child not only survives but thrives, turning obstacles into stepping-stones on their journey to becoming their best self.

KEY TAKEAWAYS

- **ADHD is a legitimate, biologically based condition**: It is not caused by "bad" parenting or a lack of discipline.
- **Myths about ADHD can be harmful**: Addressing misconceptions helps shift focus toward practical support and understanding.
- **Neurodiversity is a strength**: ADHD traits such as creativity, empathy, and adaptability can become powerful tools when nurtured.
- **Understanding the neuroscience of ADHD empowers parents**: Metaphors like the "brain as a

city" simplify complex ideas and equip parents with actionable strategies.
- **Recognize the subtle ADHD symptoms**: Understanding the impact of time blindness and social misunderstandings is crucial for early and effective support.
- **ADHD impacts family dynamics**: Encouraging family-wide solutions and fostering open communication creates a resilient and supportive environment.
- **ADHD evolves**: Awareness of how traits manifest differently in early childhood, school years, and adolescence enables tailored parenting strategies.
- **Celebrating strengths while addressing challenges**: Identifying your child's unique abilities helps them embrace ADHD as part of their identity.

By understanding ADHD and applying this knowledge with compassion and flexibility, you provide your child with the foundation they need to thrive in a world that often misunderstands them.

WHAT'S NEXT?

Now that you understand ADHD and its impact on your child, it's time to build the kind of empathetic connection that sets the stage for effective parenting. In the next chapter, you'll learn practical strategies to improve communication, build trust, and strengthen emotional intelligence in your child.

TWO
BUILDING EMPATHY AND CONNECTION

I magine stepping into your child's sneakers for a day, feeling the world as they do, every sensation magnified, every sound a symphony of distraction. You're in a classroom, a place that should be calm and focused, but instead, it's a whirlwind of noise. The hum of fluorescent lights, the scratch of pencils on paper, and the whispers of classmates drown out the teacher's voice. You sit there, trying to concentrate, but the sensory overload is overwhelming. Your mind flits from one thought to another, like a butterfly in a field of wildflowers, never settling long enough to absorb what's being taught.

Then, reality hits. You glance around and realize that everyone else is flipping through their textbooks or jotting down notes—they're clearly keeping up. Panic sets in as you recognize you haven't processed anything the teacher has said. Suddenly, the teacher calls your name, asking you to summarize the last point discussed—your heart pounds as you stare at her, completely lost. The words tumble out awkwardly, and you see a few classmates smirk. The moment feels crushing, and you wonder why keeping up seems so effortless for everyone else but impossible for you.

This chapter guides you through strategies for building empathy and connection to truly grasp the overwhelming and often isolating experiences faced by your child with ADHD. From creating a haven of emotional safety to mastering active listening and honing communication techniques, these approaches aim to fortify the bond between you and your child. With some minor adjustments, daily challenges can become opportunities for connection and understanding.

CREATING A SAFE EMOTIONAL ENVIRONMENT AT HOME

Creating a home that feels like a haven is crucial for a child with ADHD. It's about establishing an emotional sanctuary where they feel accepted and supported, no matter what storms rage outside. This involves fostering a climate of unconditional acceptance—letting your child know that their worth is not tied to their achievements or failures. Imagine a space where open dialogue flows naturally and conversations can dig deep without fear of reprimand. In this environment, your child learns that expressing their feelings is safe and welcome, even when those feelings are difficult to articulate.

Building this emotional sanctuary also means being intentional about how you respond to your child's struggles. When they face meltdowns or moments of frustration, approaching them with patience and understanding rather than criticism reinforces their sense of security. Instead of saying, "Why can't you just calm down?" try, "I can see this is hard for you. Let's figure out a way to make it easier." Such language soothes the immediate tension and models empathy, showing your child how to approach challenges with kindness toward themselves and others.

Six Practical Tips for Creating a Safe Emotional Environment:

1. **Engage in Daily Emotional Check-ins:** Set aside 10 minutes each evening to discuss the highs and lows of the day using prompts like "What was your favorite part of today?" or "What was something challenging you faced?"

2. **Establish Rituals for Connection:** Create predictable routines such as family movie nights, bedtime stories, or shared meals to foster a sense of stability.
3. **Set Clear Expectations:** Use a visual chart or list of family rules and routines to help children understand boundaries and expectations.
4. **Designate a Calm Space:** Provide a quiet area in your home where your child can decompress when overwhelmed, stocked with calming items like pillows, sensory toys, or coloring materials.
5. **Reinforce Positive Behavior:** Celebrate small victories with verbal praise or rewards to build confidence and encourage positive actions.
6. **Offer comfort by physical touch:** A hug after a meltdown or a gentle hand on their shoulder during homework struggles, can be incredibly reassuring. These gestures remind your child that you're there for them, both physically and emotionally. This consistent presence helps them build a strong foundation of trust and security.

THE POWER OF ACTIVE LISTENING

Picture this: You're in the middle of preparing dinner, mentally juggling the day's remaining tasks, when your child approaches with a story about their day. Active listening, in its essence, is the art of setting aside your thoughts and focusing entirely on the speaker. It demands your attention like a captivating novel you can't put down. At this moment, you have a choice: to brush off their words with a distracted "mhm" or to tune in, offering them your true undivided attention. Choosing the latter signals to your child that what they have to say matters deeply to you and brings a sense of joy and connection to the conversation.

This act of presence goes beyond just hearing words; it aims to understand the emotions and thoughts behind them. When you stop stirring the pot, turn off the burner, and kneel to their level, your child feels the warmth of being seen and valued. Active listening requires resisting the urge to rush in with solutions or interruptions. Create a safe space where their thoughts can unfold naturally, even if their story meanders into tales of talking sandwiches or playground adventures. Over time, these moments of genuine connection build trust and foster a deeper emotional bond between you and your child.

Five Steps to Active Listening:

1. **Give Your Full Attention**: Pause what you are doing, maintain eye contact, and show with your body language that you are fully present.
2. **Reflect Back**: Paraphrase what your child is saying. For instance, "It sounds like you felt really upset when that happened."
3. **Ask Open-ended Questions**: Encourage them to elaborate with prompts like, "What happened next?" or "How did that make you feel?"
4. **Avoid Judging or Solving**: Resist the urge to offer advice immediately. Instead, validate their experience with comments like, "That sounds tough," or "I understand why you felt that way."

5. **Summarize and Reassure**: End the conversation by summarizing key points to show understanding and offering reassurance, such as, "I'm so glad you shared that with me. We can figure it out together."

COMMUNICATION STRATEGIES FOR BUILDING TRUST

Has your child ever come home upset after getting in trouble at school for not handing in their homework? You want to address the issue while maintaining their trust. Start by ensuring you are in a quiet environment—maybe sit together in a cozy spot, away from distractions (and eavesdropping siblings). Begin the conversation by acknowledging their feelings: "I can see you're upset. Do you want to tell me what happened?" This opening shows you're not jumping to conclusions and that you're genuinely interested in hearing their side of the story.

Once your child starts sharing, use child-friendly language to explain the situation in a way that makes them feel supported rather than judged. For instance, "I know sometimes it's hard to keep track of everything, especially when a lot is going on. Not handing in homework doesn't mean you're not trying; it just means we might need to find a better system to help you stay on top of things." Avoid placing blame, as this can create defensiveness. Instead, focus on problem-solving collaboratively, which helps your child feel empowered rather than criticized.

Collaborative problem-solving approaches, like brainstorming ideas together, can strengthen your bond. For example, "What do you think would help you remember to hand in your homework? Maybe we could try setting a reminder on your tablet or using a checklist?" By involving your child in creating solutions, you teach them valuable decision-making and planning skills that can serve them well beyond the immediate challenge.

Nonverbal communication is equally vital in building trust. Maintaining eye contact during these discussions shows your child they have your full attention. A calm tone and open body language reinforces your approachability, making it easier for them to share openly. Sometimes, a reassuring gesture—like a hand on their shoulder—can speak volumes about your support and understanding, especially during emotionally charged moments.

Over time, consistency in how you communicate helps establish reliability and predictability in your relationship. Regular family check-ins or one-on-one chats create opportunities to address concerns and celebrate successes. These moments help build a foundation of trust and understanding, where your child knows they can turn to you for support without fear of judgment.

TEACHING EMPATHY AND EMOTIONAL REGULATION TO YOUR CHILD

Emotional intelligence is the ability to perceive, understand, and manage emotions—a critical skill for children with ADHD. Imagine your child navigating a world filled with highs and lows, using their excitement as a catalyst for creativity in art class, or channeling frustration into solving a challenging puzzle. Empathy and emotional regulation, when nurtured, can transform their social landscape, enabling them to form deeper connections and approach interactions with greater confidence.

Developing emotional intelligence also helps children manage the misunderstandings they might face. For instance, if your child reacts strongly to a minor incident, others may misinterpret their emotions. Teaching them to recognize and articulate their feelings can clarify misunderstandings and build bridges in social situations. These skills not only enhance their interpersonal relationships but also provide them with tools to navigate the complexities of their other ADHD-related struggles, such as impulsivity, reactivity, emotional outbursts, or difficulty reading social cues.

One powerful way to teach empathy and emotional intelligence is through role-playing. For example, if your child struggles with sharing toys, you can act out scenarios where they practice taking turns. Use playful language and exaggerated expressions to make the exercise engaging. Afterward, discuss how the other person might feel during the interaction and brainstorm ways to handle similar real-life situations. These role-playing sessions teach empathy and help children build confidence in managing social challenges.

Storytelling is another effective method. Choose books or movies with strong emotional themes and discuss the characters' feelings and actions. Ask your child questions like, "Why do you think the character felt that way?" or "What could they have done differently?" These discussions encourage your child to think about emotions from multiple perspectives, fostering a deeper understanding of empathy and emotional responses.

Finally, as a parent, modeling emotional intelligence in your daily interactions is crucial. When you openly discuss your feelings and demonstrate healthy coping mechanisms, your child learns by example. For instance, if you're feeling stressed, you might say, "I'm feeling overwhelmed right now, so I'm going to take a few deep breaths to calm down." This transparency normalizes emotional expression and shows your child that it's okay to have complex feelings as long as they're managed constructively.

Five Activities to Build Emotional Intelligence:

Here are practical activities backed by research to support your child's emotional development:

1. **Emotion Wheel Exercise**
   - Why it's useful: Studies show that children who can identify and label their emotions are better at regulating them. ADHD brains process emotions intensely, making it essential to practice recognizing feelings.
   - How to do it: Print or create an emotion wheel with a variety of feelings (e.g., happy, sad, frustrated, excited, overwhelmed). Throughout the day, sit down with your child and ask them to point to or name how they feel in that moment. Discuss what caused the emotion and how they responded.
   - Example: After a tough day at school, ask, "Which emotion on the wheel best matches how you feel?" Then, talk about what happened and

brainstorm ways to handle similar emotions in the future.

2. **Empathy Charades**
   - Why it's useful: Many ADHD children struggle with recognizing emotions in others. Acting out feelings helps them develop social awareness in a fun, engaging way.
   - How to do it: Take turns acting out different emotions without using words while the other person guesses the feeling. Discuss what clues (facial expressions, body language) helped identify the emotion.
   - Example: Act out "excited" by jumping up and clapping. Ask, "What might make someone feel this way?"

3. **Story Discussions**
   - Why it's useful: ADHD children often struggle with emotional reasoning in real time. Books provide a structured way to explore emotions at a slower, more reflective pace.
   - How to do it: Read books with emotional themes and pause to discuss how the characters feel. Ask open-ended questions like, "Why do you think they felt that way?" or "What would you do in this situation?"
   - Example: While reading a story about friendship, ask, "How do you think this character felt when they were left out?" and brainstorm ways to handle similar feelings.

4. **Model Empathy in Everyday Life**
   - Why it's useful: Children learn best through observation. When parents openly express

emotions and coping strategies, kids mirror these behaviors.
- How to do it: Narrate your emotions in an age-appropriate way and demonstrate problem-solving techniques.
- Example: "I felt really frustrated when I lost my keys earlier, but I took a deep breath, retraced my steps, and found them. That helped me stay calm."

5. **Practice Gratitude Daily**
    - Why it's useful: Research shows that gratitude helps with emotional resilience, which is especially important for children with ADHD who may experience frequent frustration or disappointment.
    - How to do it: Each night before bed, take turns sharing one thing you are grateful for. This simple routine shifts focus to positive emotions and strengthens emotional connections.
    - Example: "Today, I'm grateful that we played outside together." Encourage your child to reflect on something good from their day.

By incorporating these activities into your daily routine, you can help your child build the emotional intelligence skills they need to navigate challenges with greater confidence and empathy.

INSIGHTS FROM THE THERAPY ROOM

In my years of working with children with ADHD and their families, one story stands out vividly. A family came to me feeling exasperated and disconnected. Their 10-year-old son,

Max, had been labeled "defiant" and "disruptive" at school. Conflicts over simple tasks like cleaning up toys or getting ready for bed had become daily battles at home. Max's parents felt at a loss, unable to understand why he seemed to resist their every effort to guide him.

During our sessions, I helped them to reframe Max's "bad behavior." Instead of seeing it as intentional defiance, I helped his parents view it through the lens of ADHD—a condition that made it hard for Max to regulate his impulses and emotions. We discussed neuroscience in simple terms: "Max's brain sometimes struggles to moderate its impulses. It's like he's driving a car with a supercharged engine but weak brakes." This analogy resonated deeply with the family. Max's parents began to see his actions not as deliberate misbehavior but as a reflection of his struggles with self-control. This shift in perspective was transformative. They moved from frustration to empathy, realizing that Max wasn't trying to be difficult—he was navigating challenges he didn't fully understand himself.

We then worked on improving communication. Instead of issuing commands like, "Why can't you just do what I ask?" they practiced saying, "Max, I know it's hard to stop playing, but let's figure out a way together to make clean-up time easier." This collaborative approach reduced conflict and gave Max a sense of agency over his actions.

Over time, Max's parents began celebrating his strengths—his creativity, sense of humor, and boundless energy. This shift improved Max's self-esteem and strengthened the family's bond. Max started approaching challenges more resiliently, knowing that his parents were his allies, not his critics.

CHAPTER REFLECTION

Building empathy and connection is a journey, not a destination. Creating a home where your child feels safe and valued, practicing active listening, and teaching emotional intelligence lays the foundation for a strong and supportive relationship. It is not always easy, but every small step strengthens your bond with your child and fosters mutual growth.

KEY TAKEAWAYS

- **Emotional safety is foundational**: Create a supportive environment where your child feels heard and valued.
- **Active listening strengthens bonds**: Giving your child your full attention fosters trust and understanding.
- **Empathy starts with you**: Model emotional intelligence and teach your child to recognize and manage feelings.
- **Collaborative communication builds trust**: Work with your child to solve problems and navigate challenges.
- **Stories connect and inspire**: Sharing your own experiences with your child offers reassurance and fresh perspectives.

By following these strategies, you'll build a strong foundation for your relationship with your child, rooted in understanding and mutual growth.

WHAT'S NEXT?

Empathy and connection are crucial, but how do you translate these into day-to-day interactions? The next chapter equips you with the tools to handle everyday parenting challenges calmly and confidently.

THREE
NAVIGATING DAILY CHALLENGES WITH CONFIDENCE AND CALM

Picture this: It's Monday morning, and chaos unfolds before your eyes. Your child refuses to put on their school uniform, breakfast sits untouched, and every gentle reminder feels like a battle. The clock ticks away, and suddenly, panic sets in—you're both still in pajamas, rushing out the door in a whirlwind of frustration. Sound familiar?

Now, imagine a different morning—one with structure. A predictable routine is in place: a visual schedule on the fridge, a checklist by the door, and a timer that signals each transition. Your child knows what comes next, reducing resistance and last-minute scrambling. Instead of frantic coaxing, they move smoothly from one task to the next, guided by a familiar rhythm.

Navigating daily challenges with a child who has ADHD is not easy. It involves creating a stable foundation of routines, managing transitions thoughtfully, addressing impulsive behaviors proactively, and celebrating their unique strengths. This section introduces practical strategies to bring structure to your child's day, such as visual schedules, interactive tools, and calming techniques. It also explores ways to make transitions smoother, reinforce desired behaviors through positive feedback and token systems, and use strength-based parenting to foster resilience and self-esteem. These tools empower both you and your child to approach each day with greater confidence, patience, and connection.

Let's explore the practical ways you can bring more calm and confidence into each day.

CREATING A SAFE EMOTIONAL ENVIRONMENT WITH ROUTINES

Creating a safe and predictable home environment is one of the most supportive things you can do for your child with ADHD. Routines offer the stability and consistency they need, which can help reduce anxiety and improve focus.

With structure, your child is less likely to feel overwhelmed by the unpredictable nature of the world around them and more able to navigate their day confidently.

Six Strategies to Ensure Successful Routines

1. **Create Morning and Evening Schedules to Add Structure and Reduce Decision Fatigue**
   - **How to Implement:** Use visual charts or checklists to outline key tasks (e.g., getting dressed, eating breakfast, brushing teeth). Make them easy to read, with colorful pictures.
   - **Make It Fun:** Involve your child in designing the chart by letting them choose the colors or decorate it. Use "to-do" and "done" checkboxes to give them a sense of accomplishment.
   - **Why It Works:** Visual schedules provide a clear roadmap for daily expectations, helping children with ADHD stay on track without constant verbal reminders.
2. **Involve Your Child in Planning to Increase Cooperation and Buy-In**
   - **How to Implement:** Sit down together and discuss the day's plan. Allow your child to provide input on activities and when they need breaks.
   - **Make It Fun:** Use stickers or small rewards for completing tasks, or set small incentives like, *"If you're dressed by 8:00 AM, you can choose the family breakfast."*
   - **Why It Works:** When children have a say in their routine, they feel more in control and are more motivated to follow through.

3. **Use Timers and Alarms to Improve Transitions and Time Awareness**
    - **How to Implement:** Set alarms or use visual timers to signal when it's time to transition from one task to another (e.g., "When this timer goes off, it's time to clean up the toys").
    - **Make It Fun:** Choose timers with animated countdowns or fun sounds. Some apps feature characters that make time management feel like a game.
    - **Why It Works:** Timers create external, predictable signals that help children transition smoothly without resistance, reducing power struggles and last-minute rushing.
4. **Build in Flexible Buffer Times to Reduce Stress and Prevent Rushing**
    - **How to Implement:** Add extra time for tasks that might take longer, such as an additional 10 minutes for getting ready or a short break between transitions.
    - **Make It Fun:** Turn buffer times into "flexibility moments" by incorporating quick, enjoyable activities like a 30-second dance break or a short storytelling session.
    - **Why It Works:** Extra time prevents the routine from feeling rushed, allowing children with ADHD to transition at their own pace while reducing frustration and anxiety.
5. **Design a Calm Space for Emotional Regulation and Self-Soothing**
    - **How to Implement:** Create a designated quiet area where your child can retreat when feeling

overwhelmed. Equip it with soft pillows, a cozy blanket, or noise-canceling headphones.
- **Make It Fun:** Let your child personalize their calm space with favorite sensory-friendly items, such as stuffed animals, fidget toys, or dimmable lights.
- **Why It Works:** Having a dedicated space for self-regulation helps children manage overwhelming emotions, reducing emotional outbursts and increasing their ability to refocus.

6. **Consistent Rituals**
   - **How to Implement**: When you create your schedules, make sure the very first morning ritual and very last evening ritual include an activity that your child can look forward to. For instance, start the day with soft music or a favorite song and end it with a calming activity like a bedtime story or a warm bath.
   - **How to Make it Fun**: Make the rituals part of a longer routine, such as having a "wake-up dance party" with fun music or a "good night song" that signals it's time to wind down.
   - **Why It Works**: Consistent rituals create familiarity and can reduce anxiety.

By integrating these structured yet flexible strategies, parents can create a predictable environment that supports their child's emotional and cognitive needs while making daily routines smoother and more enjoyable

MANAGING MORNING AND EVENING TRANSITIONS

While routines provide a sense of structure, transitioning from one activity to another can still be challenging for children with ADHD. This could include moving from sleeping to waking or from playtime to homework. These changes can overwhelm your child, leading to frustration and resistance. However, some thoughtful strategies can make transitions smoother and more predictable.

Three Strategies for Smoother Transitions:

1. **Calming Techniques**:
   - **How to Implement**: Teach your child a calming technique, such as deep breathing or stretching, to help them feel grounded during transitions. Practice these techniques with them every day so they become a regular part of the routine.
   - **How to Make it Fun**: Give the breathing exercises fun names, like "balloon breaths" or "pretend to blow out candles." Let your child visualize their favorite calm place while practicing the technique.
   - **Why It Works**: Deep breathing and stretching techniques activate the body's relaxation response, helping your child manage the physical and emotional shifts during transitions.
2. **Use Rewards Systems for Positive Reinforcement**:
   - **How to Implement**: Use rewards to reinforce successful transitions. For example, create a reward chart where your child earns a sticker for each successful transition (e.g., from getting up to

getting dressed, or from playing to doing homework).
- **How to Make it Fun**: Let your child choose the reward system, like stickers, coins, or stars. Let them help decide what rewards they would like to earn, such as extra screen time or a fun outing.
- **Why It Works**: Positive reinforcement motivates your child to engage in the behaviors you want to see more of. Immediate rewards help reinforce the behavior and make transitions feel rewarding.

3. **Interactive Tools**:
   - **How to Implement**: If your child struggles with transitions, offer sensory tools, like weighted blankets or soft toys, for a brief time (2 to 5 minutes) to help them adjust. You can also use specific apps designed for mindfulness or relaxation.
   - **How to Make it Fun**: Incorporate these tools into a "transition kit" that your child can take with them. For example, they might carry a favorite toy or a calming sensory object that they use when transitioning.
   - **Why It Works**: Sensory tools can calm the body and provide a tangible, soothing outlet when your child feels anxious or overwhelmed. This support helps them feel more in control during transitions.

HANDLING IMPULSIVE BEHAVIORS IN PUBLIC SETTINGS

Once your child feels comfortable with transitions at home, you can focus on helping them manage impulsive behaviors in public settings, such as at the grocery store or in a busy park. These moments can be overstimulating and may trigger impulsive actions. However, with the proactive strategies outlined below, you can turn these potentially challenging moments into lessons in patience, self-awareness, or self-regulation.

Three Proactive Techniques for Managing Impulsivity:

1. **Prepare with Social Stories**:

Social stories are short, structured narratives that help children understand and navigate social situations, expectations, and emotions. Originally developed by Carol Gray for children with autism, social stories have also proven highly effective for children with ADHD, who often struggle with impulse control, perspective-taking, and social interactions.

Social stories use clear, simple language and/or pictures to describe real-life situations step by step, helping children visualize appropriate responses and behaviors. Research suggests that structured storytelling enhances cognitive flexibility and emotional regulation in children with ADHD by providing concrete examples of expected behaviors in various situations; children who use social stories demonstrate improved self-awareness, better peer interactions, and reduced anxiety in social settings.

For example, a social story about "Waiting My Turn to Speak" might describe a scenario where a child is in class, feels excited to share an idea, but learns how to raise their hand, wait, and listen to others before speaking. By reading and discussing these stories regularly, children with ADHD can internalize social norms and practice self-regulation in a way that feels engaging and supportive rather than overwhelming

- **Implementation**: Use social stories to walk your child through the expected behaviors before going out. For example, to help explain that they will need to wait in line or use their indoor voice when in public.
- **How to Make it Fun**: Create the social story with your child using pictures or drawings. This makes it feel more like a collaborative experience and helps them internalize the expectations.
- **Why It Works**: Social stories give your child a clear framework for behavior and a mental picture of what will happen, reducing anxiety and impulsivity. They are especially useful in the lead-up to activities that are unfamiliar or anxiety-provoking.

2. **Role-Play Scenarios**:

- **Implementation**: Before heading out, role-play situations that might be challenging, like waiting in line, asking for help, or handling disappointment. Do this at home so your child can practice.
- **How to Make it Fun**: Turn role-playing into a game. Let your child play the role of the shopper or

customer while you play the role of the cashier. This creates an interactive experience where your child can practice the expected behavior.
- **Why It Works**: Role-playing gives your child a script to follow when encountering similar situations in public, boosting their confidence and self-control.

3. **Distraction Tools**:

- **Implementation**: Bring a "transition bag" filled with distractions like drawing games, coloring books, or fidget toys. These items can help your child focus and calm down during overstimulating moments.
- **How to Make it Fun**: Let your child pick out the items for the bag and rotate the contents regularly so that they remain interested. You can add a few small surprise items to make the bag feel like a special resource.
- **Why It Works**: Distraction tools provide a calming outlet and help your child redirect their energy in a positive direction, making it easier to manage impulsivity in public places.

POSITIVE REINFORCEMENT: ENCOURAGING DESIRED BEHAVIORS

Positive reinforcement is one of the most effective tools for encouraging desired behaviors. By offering immediate and meaningful rewards for positive actions, you motivate your child to repeat these behaviors, which can build their confidence and self-regulation.

Three Tips to Implement Positive Reinforcement:

1. **Immediate Feedback**:
   - **Implementation**: Whenever your child engages in the desired behavior (e.g., sharing with a sibling, staying seated at the table), immediately provide positive verbal feedback, such as "Great job!" or "I'm so proud of you!"
   - **How to Make it Fun**: Incorporate fun phrases, songs, or cheers to make the feedback more engaging. For example, you could say, "You did it! You're a star!" or sing a little "Great job!" song.
   - **Why It Works**: Immediate praise strengthens the connection between the action and the reward, reinforcing the behavior.
2. **Token Systems**:
   - **Implementation**: Create a token system where your child earns tokens for completing tasks or demonstrating positive behaviors. These tokens can be exchanged for a reward, such as extra screen time or a special outing. For example, your child might earn a token for each morning they get dressed on time or each time they finish homework without reminders. Tip: choose tokens that will motivate your child, e.g., stickers of superheroes or colorful marbles.
   - **How to Make it Fun**: Let your child decorate a "reward chart" or "reward jar" and add their tokens (e.g., stickers or marbles) to it. Set a goal for the number of tokens needed for a reward and let them choose the reward.

- **Why It Works**: A token system provides an external, tangible way to reinforce positive behaviors and visually gives your child something to work toward. However, the following tips will make sure that your token system works:
3. **Fading Rewards Gradually**:
    - **Implementation**: As the behavior becomes more ingrained, reduce the frequency of tangible rewards (like tokens or treats) and shift to verbal praise or recognition. For example, instead of giving a token every time they get dressed, start sharing it after every third time.
    - **How to Make it Fun**: Celebrate milestones with a special reward, such as a family outing or a favorite activity, when your child hits a significant achievement, like going a whole week without needing reminders to clean their room.
    - **Why It Works**: Gradually reducing external rewards encourages intrinsic motivation, which helps your child develop a sense of pride and satisfaction in their actions.

BUILDING RESILIENCE THROUGH STRENGTH-BASED PARENTING

Strength-based parenting shifts the focus from deficiencies to capabilities, and promotes the development of resilience, self-esteem, and a growth mindset. When you celebrate your child's talents, whether they are artistic, athletic, or social, you help them build a sense of identity that is rooted in their strengths rather than their struggles.

Four Ways to Foster Your Child's Strengths:

1. **Encourage Creative Expression**:
   - **Implementation**: Provide outlets for your child to express themselves creatively. This might include drawing, painting, music, or building with blocks. These activities allow your child to tap into their natural talents, build confidence, and experience joy in their accomplishments.
   - **How to Make it Fun**: Create art projects together or participate in a family talent show where your child can showcase their creative skills. This makes creativity feel like a shared experience and gives them a platform to shine.
   - **Why It Works**: Creative expression fosters a sense of accomplishment and self-worth. When your child feels good about their creative abilities, it boosts their confidence and provides a healthy emotional outlet.
2. **Highlight Leadership Opportunities**:
   - **Implementation**: Provide opportunities for your child to take on leadership roles, whether helping to set the table, leading a family activity, or being the "line leader" at school. This allows them to feel valued and capable.
   - **How to Make it Fun**: Set up family projects where your child can lead, like organizing a game night or planning a family outing. They will feel proud to take the lead and make decisions.
   - **Why It Works**: Leadership opportunities build a sense of responsibility and accomplishment,

boosting your child's self-esteem and reinforcing their ability to influence the world around them.

3. **Promote a Growth Mindset:**
   - **Implementation**: Encourage your child to view setbacks as opportunities for growth. Help them understand that making mistakes is part of learning and improvement. Praise their effort rather than just the outcome.
   - **How to Make it Fun**: Turn challenges into games, such as setting goals and celebrating progress. For example, if they're learning to read, challenge them to read more each day and celebrate each new word they master.
   - **Why It Works**: A growth mindset fosters resilience and perseverance. Focusing on effort rather than innate ability empowers your child to keep trying and learning, even when faced with difficulties.

4. **Incorporate Physical Activity**:
   - **Implementation**: Physical activities like sports, dance, or outdoor play can channel your child's energy positively while teaching discipline, teamwork, and perseverance. These activities are suitable for physical health and emotional well-being.
   - **How to Make it Fun**: Try activities your child enjoys, such as running races, playing sports, or having a dance-off. The more fun and engaging the physical activity, the more your child will look forward to it.
   - **Why It Works**: Physical activity helps release pent-up energy, improve focus, and foster

teamwork, all of which contributes to greater emotional resilience and physical health.

INSIGHTS FROM THE THERAPY ROOM

I have often seen how collaboration and a structured approach can transform challenges into manageable—and even rewarding—experiences. I recall working with a family who came to me feeling overwhelmed by their daughter's impulsive outbursts, particularly during public outings. Together, we developed a tailored behavior modification plan that addressed specific challenges by reinforcing positive behaviors and reducing undesired ones.

The first step was to identify patterns. Through conversations and observations, we realized that overstimulation in crowded environments often led to their daughter's impulsive behaviors. With this insight, we introduced proactive strategies. For instance, the parents created and started using visual social stories at home to prepare their daughter for what he could expect during outings. They also equipped her with sensory tools, like a small fidget toy, to provide a soothing outlet when she felt overstimulated.

It was crucial to involve their daughter in the process. During a family meeting, she shared her feelings about these outings and contributed ideas, such as taking short breaks in quieter areas when she began to feel overwhelmed. This collaboration empowered her and gave her a sense of control over her environment.

The family also embraced positive reinforcement. Each time their daughter successfully managed her impulses—whether by waiting patiently or using polite words—she earned a token that could be exchanged for a favorite activity. Over time, these small wins accumulated, boosting her confidence and reinforcing the value of effort.

What stood out most was the transformation in how the parents perceived their daughter's behaviors. Initially viewed as defiance, they began understanding these actions as responses to environmental and emotional triggers. This shift in perspective fostered greater empathy, enabling them to approach challenges with patience and compassion.

Ultimately, the plan's success lies in the strategies implemented and the family's commitment to working together. Watching their daughter thrive in situations that once felt insurmountable was a testament to the power of collaboration, understanding, and structured support. These moments of growth and connection remind me why this work is so profoundly rewarding.

CHAPTER REFLECTION

Parenting a child with ADHD requires balancing structure with flexibility, consistency, and adaptability. Establishing routines, managing transitions, addressing impulsive behaviors, and celebrating strengths lay a foundation for your child's growth and self-confidence. Each strategy, whether through positive reinforcement, resilience-building, or strength-based parenting, provides you with practical tools to support your child's development. When woven into your daily life, these tools help your child navigate challenges and create a deeper connection and understanding within your family.

KEY TAKEAWAYS

1. **Routines provide a stable foundation**: They reduce anxiety and enhance focus by creating a predictable environment.
2. **Smooth transitions ease daily life**: Use calming techniques and positive reinforcement to help your child navigate transitions easily.
3. **Proactive strategies reduce impulsivity**: Turn public outings into teachable moments with preparation and sensory tools.
4. **Positive reinforcement motivates desired behaviors**: Reinforce desired behaviors through praise, tokens, and consistency.
5. **Strength-based parenting highlights abilities**: Promoting resilience and self-esteem helps your child grow into a confident, capable individual.

Incorporating these techniques into your parenting approach empowers your child to face the world confidently and with a sense of belonging. These practical tools will help create a more harmonious and supportive family dynamic, providing a solid foundation for your child's future.

WHAT'S NEXT?

Successfully managing daily challenges often depends on your child's ability to regulate their emotions. Let's explore how to help your child develop emotional health and resilience.

FOUR
EMOTIONAL REGULATION AND WELL-BEING

It's an all-too-common scenario: You've planned a fun family outing to the park. The sun shines brightly, the picnic basket is packed with all the family's favorite treats, and your child bounces excitedly, chattering about all the games they will play. It feels like the perfect day, and you've pictured laughter, relaxation, and maybe even a peaceful moment to yourself while the kids run around. However, as soon as you arrive, things take an unexpected turn. A meltdown erupts over something seemingly minor—the wrong-colored juice box, a sibling stepping ahead in line, or the park being busier than anticipated. The idyllic scene you envisioned quickly dissolves into frustration, raised voices, and tears. You scramble to calm your child while juggling the reactions of others—your own emotions brewing just below the surface.

Scenarios like these highlight the critical role of emotional regulation for children with ADHD, for whom the ability to understand and manage emotions doesn't always come easily. However, each seemingly small, daily interaction is an opportunity to teach them skills they'll carry for life—skills that can turn moments of chaos into chances for connection and growth and lay the foundation for meaningful relationships, resilience, and self-esteem. In this chapter, we'll explore practical tools and strategies to help your child regulate their emotions, manage sensory overload, practice mindfulness, and build the confidence they need for a happier, more resilient future. Through intentional guidance and small but meaningful shifts, you can transform these everyday challenges into building blocks for emotional well-being and a stronger family bond.

EMOTIONAL REGULATION AND UNDERSTANDING TRIGGERS

Emotional regulation is a key skill for children with ADHD. It involves identifying their emotions, understanding what triggers those emotions, and learning how to respond in a balanced way. Think of emotions as different colors on a rainbow—each distinct and recognizable. The first step in emotional regulation is helping your child understand their feelings so they can begin to identify them when they occur.

Three Practical Steps to Support Emotional Regulation:

1. **Identifying Emotions**:
    - **Implementation**: Start by teaching your child how to label their emotions. For younger children, you can do this through an emotion chart or by using everyday situations to ask them how they feel. For instance, after a stressful situation, ask, "How did that make you feel? Was that frustration, sadness, or something else?" Older children can be encouraged to journal their feelings, or prompted with more advanced questions, such as, "how did that feel in your body?"
    - **How to Make it Fun**: Make it a game by using flashcards, videos from YouTube, or drawing faces that express different emotions. Help your child connect each face with a time they've felt that emotion.
    - **Why It Works**: The more your child can identify and name their emotions, the more control they'll have over how they react to them. It's the first

step toward managing emotional responses instead of being overwhelmed by them. (There are many adults who could benefit from similar activities to help them improve their emotional literacy!)
2. **Recognizing Triggers**:
    - **Implementation**: Look for patterns in your child's behavior to identify common triggers. For instance, does your child get upset when hungry, tired, or exposed to loud noises, or when they spend time with a certain peer, or have too much on their schedule?
    - **How to Make it Fun**: Create a "trigger diary" together where your child can record what happened before they felt upset. This can be as simple as drawing pictures or using stickers to mark certain events.
    - **Why It Works**: Understanding what causes emotional outbursts helps your child anticipate and avoid these triggers. Children who recognize the early signs of frustration or anger are more likely to ask for help before the situation escalates.
3. **Interactive Element: Emotion Identification Chart**:
    - **Implementation**: Create an emotion chart with your child. Use a large poster board or a printable with faces showing different emotions. Encourage your child to use it to pinpoint their feelings during or after emotional moments. For example, they might point to the "frustrated" face when they are

upset because they can't finish a puzzle. For older children, use examples connected to characters from their favorite movie or Netflix show.
- **Why It Works**: Visual cues may help your child articulate their feelings when they cannot express them verbally. This practice encourages emotional awareness and gives them an alternative means to communicate their emotions effectively.

MANAGING SENSORY OVERLOAD: TOOLS AND STRATEGIES

For children with ADHD, managing sensory overload is a crucial part of emotional regulation. Sensory overload occurs when a child is overwhelmed by too much sensory input—such as loud noises, bright lights, or crowds. Sensory overload can lead to anxiety, irritability, or emotional meltdowns. Providing tools and strategies to manage these moments helps your child regain control and feel more comfortable in overwhelming situations.

Three Practical Tools for Sensory Management:

1. **Noise-Canceling Headphones**:
    - **Implementation**: Noise-canceling headphones work by actively reducing background noise through a process called active noise cancellation (ANC). These headphones use tiny microphones to detect external sounds and generate sound waves that cancel them out before they reach the ear. Noise-cancelling headphones can be

especially helpful in crowded places like malls, airports, or busy restaurants.
- **How to Make it Fun**: Let your child choose the headphones themselves to make it feel like a fun and personal tool. You can even decorate them together with stickers that are meaningful to your child.
- **Why It Works**: Noise-canceling headphones reduce external distractions and help your child focus on the task in front of them, making overwhelming sensory experiences more manageable.

2. **Sensory Retreat at Home**:
    - **Implementation**: Create a sensory-friendly space at home where your child can retreat when overwhelmed. This might include soft lighting, calming colors, comfortable textures like plush pillows or blankets, and a quiet environment.
    - **How to Make it Fun**: Let your child help decorate the space to their liking, choosing calming objects or adding personal touches like favorite books or toys. This makes the sensory space feel special and comforting.
    - **Why It Works**: A sensory-friendly space provides your child a safe retreat to self-regulate and calm down after feeling overwhelmed. Having a consistent, comforting place to go helps them feel secure.

3. **Fidget Tools**:
    - **Implementation**: Fidget toys are small, handheld objects (such as stress balls, spinner rings, or textured pads) designed to provide sensory

stimulation and movement, helping children with ADHD manage their energy levels, improve focus, and regulate emotions. While they might seem like simple distractions, research suggests that engaging in small, repetitive motor movements can enhance concentration and self-regulation—particularly for children who struggle with hyperactivity and impulsivity. Fidget toys can help your child channel excess energy and focus during stressful situations. Keep a variety of these tools accessible at home and on the go.

- **How to Make it Fun**: Turn fidgeting into a positive habit by letting your child pick out their favorite fidget toys or letting them rotate them for variety. You can make it a game to see how many "squeezes" they can do in a row.
- **Why It Works**: Fidget toys provide tactile feedback that helps your child release nervous energy productively, promoting calmness and reducing stress. In addition, research shows that mild physical movement can increase dopamine and norepinephrine levels in the brain, neurotransmitters associated with attention and motivation. Engaging the hands with a fidget toy allows the brain to remain alert, making it easier to focus on tasks like listening in class or completing homework.

MINDFULNESS TECHNIQUES FOR CHILDREN AND PARENTS

You've probably heard of mindfulness, but what is it, really? Mindfulness is the practice of bringing full attention to the present moment with openness, curiosity, and non-judgment. Mindfulness teaches children to stay present, manage stress, and regulate emotions. Research shows that mindfulness-based interventions can significantly improve attention, impulse control, and emotional regulation in children with ADHD. Studies indicate that mindfulness strengthens neural pathways and improves executive functioning. In fact, a 2018 meta-analysis in the Journal of Child Psychology and Psychiatry found that mindfulness-based training can reduce ADHD symptoms, sometimes producing effects comparable to stimulant medication.

Beyond cognitive improvements, mindfulness has a direct impact on emotional regulation and stress reduction. Children with ADHD often experience heightened emotional reactivity due to dysregulation in the part of the brain called the amygdala, making them more prone to frustration and anxiety. Simple mindfulness techniques, such as deep breathing, bubble breathing, and mindfulness games can moderate this by lowering cortisol levels and promoting calmness. A 2019 study in Frontiers in Psychology found that children who practiced mindfulness regularly showed fewer emotional outbursts and improved social interactions.

Finally (and importantly), mindfulness fosters self-compassion, well-being, and resilience, helping children reframe negative self-perceptions and build confidence (this was the topic of my PhD research). Practical exercises like breathwork, "Five Senses Scanning," and structured mindfulness breaks can be easily incorporated into daily routines at home (and in schools), supporting children in developing greater self-awareness, emotional stability, and improved focus.

Three Practical Steps to Introduce Mindfulness to Your Child:

1. **Bubble Breathing**:
   - **Implementation**: Teach your child to use "bubble breathing" by pretending to blow bubbles. Instruct them to take a deep breath in, then slowly exhale as if they were blowing bubbles, making the "bubble" as big and slow as possible.
   - **How to Make it Fun**: Let your child practice with real bubbles or make it into a game where they try to blow the biggest bubble. The playful nature of the activity keeps the child engaged while helping them practice mindful breathing.
   - **Why It Works**: By focusing on slow, deep breaths, children activate their parasympathetic nervous system and engage in mindful breathing, which has been shown to:
     - **Lower heart rate and blood pressure** – Helps reduce physiological symptoms of stress and anxiety.
     - **Increase oxygen flow to the brain** – Supports clearer thinking, better focus, and improved impulse control.
     - **Promote mindfulness** – Encourages children to stay in the present moment, reducing distractions.
     - **Engage sensory and motor skills** – Physically blowing bubbles provides a

structured, visual way to practice breath control.

2. **Guided Imagery**:
   - **Implementation**: Use guided imagery to help your child regulate their emotions. For example, guide your child through a calming story, asking them to imagine being in a peaceful place, such as a quiet beach or a forest. Ask them to focus on details like the sounds, smells, and textures in the imagined story or scene.
   - **How to Make it Fun**: Turn guided imagery into an interactive experience. Ask your child to "create" their peaceful place with drawings or during play, allowing them to fully engage their imagination.
   - **Why It Works**: Guided imagery provides a mental escape, allowing your child to relax and disconnect from stressful or overwhelming situations. Research has shown that visualization activates the same neural pathways as real experiences, meaning that imagining a peaceful scenario can trigger actual physiological relaxation responses, such as:
     - **Lowering heart rate and blood pressure** – Helps calm physical signs of hyperactivity and anxiety.
     - **Engaging the prefrontal cortex** – Supports self-regulation and impulse control by promoting mindfulness.
     - **Increasing dopamine levels** – Enhances motivation and attention, which are often lower in children with ADHD.

- **Improving working memory** – Strengthens mental organization skills by helping children "hold onto" visual information.
3. **Interactive Element: Mindfulness Journal**:
    - **Implementation**: Create a mindfulness journal for your child to track moments in which they practiced mindfulness. This might include drawing pictures of their feelings, writing down their breathing techniques, or noting moments when they felt calm.
    - **Why It Works**: A mindfulness journal serves as a tool for reflection, helping your child visualize and internalize their mindful moments. It also builds a habit of practicing mindfulness regularly.

COGNITIVE BEHAVIORAL THERAPY AT HOME

While mindfulness techniques help children stay grounded in the present moment, promoting long-term emotional growth, it's also important to address any underlying, unhelpful thought patterns and/or behaviors. Cognitive Behavioral Therapy (CBT) helps children recognize the connections between their thoughts, emotions, and behaviors. By teaching your child how to reframe negative thoughts and their behavioral responses, you empower them to make more thoughtful, controlled decisions. CBT is one of the most popular therapeutic techniques utilized by psychologists, as it has a very high level of research to back its effectiveness. However, the concepts can easily be applied at home, too.

Practical Tools for practicing CBT at home:

1. **Stop-Think-Act**:
   - **Implementation**: Introduce the "Stop-Think-Act" strategy, where your child pauses when they start to feel upset or frustrated. They stop, take a deep breath, think about their response, and then act.
   - **How to Make it Fun**: Turn the "Stop-Think-Act" process into a game. Discuss or re-create scenarios that require them to stop and think (such as wanting to blurt out in class, or throw the pieces of a board game when they are losing) and then reward them for thinking of a more thoughtful decision. You can use a physical reminder, like a stop sign magnet on the fridge or a small card in their backpack, to reinforce the strategy.
   - **Why It Works**: This technique teaches children to interrupt impulsive behavior by inserting a structured pause before reacting, an essential skill for emotional regulation. It promotes impulse control and strengthens executive function skills by reinforcing decision-making and self-control. Furthermore, this activity encourages reflection by helping children visualize consequences before acting and builds independence and confidence by giving them a practical strategy to manage emotions and behaviors.
2. **Thought Journal**:
   - **Implementation**: Have your child keep a thought journal where they write or draw about their

thoughts, emotions, and behaviors. This habit helps them track patterns in their thinking patterns, emotional responses and actions, and work toward more productive ways of thinking and behaving.
- **How to Make it Fun**: Let your child decorate their thought journal with stickers or drawings, making it a personal and fun project. Encourage them to reflect on which thoughts are helpful (i.e., the thoughts that led them towards making positive choices) and which ones are less helpful (i.e., thoughts that feed negative emotions or behaviors).
- **Why It Works**: Keeping a thought journal helps children reflect and gain insight as to how their thoughts influence their feelings and behaviors. Over time, they can learn to reframe unhelpful thoughts into more helpful, constructive ones.

FOSTERING SOCIAL SKILLS AND FRIENDSHIPS

Social interactions can feel challenging for children with ADHD. Difficulty with impulse control, turn-taking, and communication can make building and maintaining friendships harder. However, with practice and encouragement, children can develop strong social skills and build meaningful connections with peers.

Practical Ideas for Social Skill Development:

1. **Role-Playing Social Scenarios:**
   - **Implementation:** Use role-playing to practice social interactions. You can play out scenarios like asking to join a game, sharing, or responding politely when they don't get their way. Encourage your child to try different strategies for approaching social situations.
   - **How to Make it Fun:** Turn role-playing into a skit or a puppet show. Use toys or stuffed animals to act out social scenarios, and let your child lead the play.
   - **Why It Works:** Role-playing allows your child to practice social skills in a safe environment and build confidence in their ability to navigate social situations.
2. **Group Activities and Playdates:**
   - **Implementation:** Encourage your child to participate in team sports, clubs, or group games. These structured settings provide natural opportunities for practicing social skills like turn-taking, listening, and teamwork.
   - **How to Make it Fun:** Organize playdates or family gatherings where your child can practice interacting with others in a relaxed setting. Guide as needed, but let your child take the lead in initiating interactions.
   - **Why It Works:** Group activities foster social development and provide a safe space to practice social skills. They also allow your child to make connections and build friendships with peers.

ADDRESSING ANXIETY AND BUILDING CONFIDENCE

Anxiety can be a significant barrier to emotional regulation for children with ADHD. Worries about failure, judgment, or new experiences can trigger anxiety that leads to avoidance or emotional outbursts. Helping your child address their anxieties and build confidence is key to supporting their emotional well-being.

Practical Strategies for Building Confidence and Reducing Anxiety:

1. **Worry Box**:
   - **Implementation**: Create a "worry box" where your child can write down or draw their worries and place them inside. At the end of the day, go through the worries together and discuss how they can be managed or let go.
   - **How to Make it Fun**: Let your child decorate their worry box with stickers or colors, making it a personal tool for managing anxiety.
   - **Why It Works**: The worry box provides a physical outlet for anxious thoughts and allows your child to externalize their worries. It also helps them feel empowered to control their anxieties in a healthy way.
2. **Celebrate Success and Small Wins**:
   - **Implementation**: Celebrate your child's achievements, no matter how small. Whether completing a homework assignment or speaking in front of the class, celebrate the effort and progress they make.

- **How to Make it Fun**: Use a "celebration jar" where you add a note for each success, and at the end of the week, review all the positive moments.
- **Why It Works**: Celebrating small successes builds self-esteem and helps your child recognize their strengths. It encourages them to take on new challenges with confidence.

INSIGHTS FROM THE THERAPY ROOM

How to effectively address emotional regulation challenges in children with ADHD is one of the questions I get asked the most. One case that stands out involved a 12-year-old girl named Emily, who was experiencing frequent emotional outbursts, particularly when interacting with her younger sibling, Lily. Emily would often become frustrated or angry over seemingly minor issues—such as Lily borrowing her things without asking or taking too long to get ready when they were supposed to leave for an event.

Emily's parents felt helpless and overwhelmed. On the other hand, Emily was frustrated by her inability to control her emotions during these moments, which often resulted in yelling or physical outbursts. This dynamic was beginning to strain the sibling relationship and cause tension in the family. We worked on several strategies to help Emily regulate her emotions and improve her interactions with Lily.

We began by helping Emily identify her emotions using an emotion chart. At first, Emily found it difficult to pinpoint exactly what she was feeling in the heat of the moment, so we spent time labeling emotions outside of the stressful situations. Over time, she started recognizing that many of her outbursts stemmed from frustration or a sense of injustice—when she felt like Lily was taking advantage of her. Emily learned how to express her feelings verbally by saying, "I feel frustrated when Lily takes my things without asking," instead of reacting impulsively.

Next, we explored Emily's emotional triggers. We identified that her frustration would often peak when she was already feeling stressed or overwhelmed—such as when doing homework or dealing with changes in her routine. By tracking these moments, we could better predict when her emotional responses might be more intense, helping Emily become more aware of the conditions that led to her outbursts.

We also worked on a "Stop-Think-Act" strategy to help Emily pause before reacting. This was especially important during interactions with Lily. Whenever Emily felt her frustration building, she would stop, take a deep breath, and think about her response before acting. We practiced role-playing scenarios where Emily could practice asking for space or calmly asking Lily to respect her belongings.

In addition, Emily's parents introduced a "calming space" in the home, where both Emily and Lily could retreat when tensions rose. Emily could use this space to regain her composure, practicing deep breathing or reading a book to calm herself down before re-engaging with Lily. This gave her a sense of control and space to reset, which was crucial in managing her emotional responses.

Over time, Emily became more aware of her emotions and learned healthier ways to cope with her frustration. She was able to communicate more calmly with Lily, and their relationship improved. Emily's parents also felt more confident supporting her, using the "Stop-Think-Act" strategy to model and reinforce positive responses.

Working with this family really reinforced to me the importance of teaching children emotional awareness and providing them the tools for self-regulation. Consistent support from both parents and siblings also helped immensely. With the right tools and strategies, children with ADHD like Emily can learn to manage their emotions more effectively, improving their relationships and overall emotional well-being.

CHAPTER REFLECTION

For children with ADHD, learning how to better identify, understand, and manage emotions can be a transformative process. As a parent or caregiver, by supporting your child in developing these skills, you provide them with the tools they need to navigate life's challenges. This journey isn't about perfection—it's about progress. There will be setbacks, and there will be breakthroughs. With patience, encouragement, and a steady approach, your child will begin to build resilience, emotional awareness, and confidence, helping them thrive in an often-overwhelming world.

By introducing tools like emotion identification, sensory management, mindfulness techniques, and Cognitive Behavioral Therapy (CBT), you're helping your child develop a deeper understanding of themselves and their emotional world. Each strategy equips your child to cope with the ups and downs of life in a way that promotes personal growth and meaningful connections with others.

Celebrate even small moments of emotional awareness, whether recognizing the first signs of frustration, taking a deep breath before reacting, or finding the right words to express feelings. With your ongoing support, and thoughtful reinforcement, your child will be well on their way to mastering their emotions, building stronger relationships, and enjoying a more balanced, fulfilling life.

KEY TAKEAWAYS

- **Emotional regulation begins with identifying emotions and recognizing triggers**: Help your child learn to name their feelings and understand what sets them off. This awareness is the first step in managing emotional responses.
- **Managing sensory overload helps children feel calm and in control of their environment**: Tools like noise-canceling headphones, sensory-friendly spaces, and fidget toys help children cope with overwhelming stimuli.
- **Mindfulness strategies provide tools for calm, focus, and stress reduction**: Practices like bubble breathing, guided imagery, and mindfulness journaling teach children how to stay grounded and reduce anxiety.
- **Cognitive Behavioral Therapy (CBT) teaches children to manage their thoughts, emotions, and behaviors**: Techniques like "Stop-Think-Act" and thought journaling help children break the cycle of impulsive reactions and make thoughtful, positive choices.

- **Social skills can be nurtured through role-playing, team activities, and gentle coaching**: Role-playing social scenarios and providing structured group activities teach children essential skills like turn-taking, cooperation, and communication.
- **Confidence grows through small successes, affirmations, and celebrating strengths**: By recognizing and celebrating achievements—big or small—your child will develop a stronger sense of self-worth and the courage to face challenges confidently.

By consistently using these strategies and staying patient throughout the process, you will help your child build the skills to manage their emotions, regulate their behavior, and ultimately lead a more confident, resilient, and fulfilling life.

WHAT'S NEXT?

The strategies shared so far are invaluable, but how can you implement them without overspending? The next chapter highlights cost-effective tools and resources to help you stay on track.

MAKE A DIFFERENCE WITH YOUR REVIEW
UNLOCK THE POWER OF CONNECTION

"The best way to find yourself is to lose yourself in the service of others."

MAHATMA GANDHI

Parenting a child with ADHD is a journey filled with ups, downs, and moments of discovery. You've taken a big step by reading *The Complete Guide to Parenting Your Child with ADHD: Proven Stress-Free Solutions to Build Confidence, Connection, and Consistency at Home and School*. Now, you can help others take that same step.

Would you help someone like you—standing in the same kitchen, staring at the same mountain of challenges, unsure where to begin?

My mission is to empower parents with the tools, understanding, and confidence they need to support their child with ADHD. But to reach more families, I need your help.

Most parents choose books based on reviews. By sharing your thoughts, you're opening the door for another family to feel seen, supported, and hopeful. Your review could be the reason they take that first step.

A few kind words can:

- Help a parent turn frustration into understanding.
- Encourage a family to see their child's potential instead of their challenges.
- Spread hope to those feeling overwhelmed and alone.

It costs nothing, takes only a moment, and can transform someone's parenting journey.

To make a difference, simply scan the QR code below or visit this link to leave a review:

https://www.amazon.com/review/create-review/?asin=B0DY9KG561

If this book has helped you in any way, your review could help it find its way into the hands of someone who truly needs it.

From the bottom of my heart, thank you for your kindness and generosity. Together, we can create a ripple effect of understanding and support for parents everywhere.

Warm regards,

- Dr. Victoria Barclay-Timmis

FIVE
COST-EFFECTIVE RESOURCES AND STRATEGIES

The cost-of-living crisis is real. Finding ways to save money, whilst also finding tools to make life easier for your child with ADHD, can be a difficult challenge. Luckily, supporting a child with ADHD doesn't have to come with a hefty price tag. In this chapter, you'll discover budget-friendly tools, DIY strategies, community resources that empower you to support your child without financial strain, and actionable steps to address everyday challenges creatively.

The resources and strategies suggested here are not intended to replace professional therapies such as occupational therapy (OT), speech therapy, or psychology. Instead, they complement these professional treatments and extend the concepts taught in therapy into your child's everyday life. These tools are designed to reinforce and build upon the work in therapy, making those concepts accessible outside the therapy room and integrated into your daily routine.

As you move through these sections, you'll learn how to identify affordable tools, creatively repurpose everyday items, craft DIY sensory aids, and leverage community resources—all while staying within your financial means.

BUDGET-FRIENDLY TOOLS AND STRATEGIES FOR TIME MANAGEMENT

Children with ADHD often struggle with time management, staying on task, and managing transitions. Visual tools like visual timers can make these concepts more accessible and less overwhelming. Visual timers, like Time Timers, help children see time passing in a way that's easy to understand. This method is beneficial for children who struggle with the concept of abstract time and need a visual cue to gauge the passing of minutes.

Visual timers reduce the stress of transitions, making it easier for children with ADHD to switch from one task to another. Instead of hearing a ticking clock or an abrupt verbal reminder to "finish up," a child can see the time slip away in real time, which allows them to mentally prepare for the transition. Many families find that visual timers help decrease the anxiety children often experience when time constraints become clear.

For a more affordable option, check online platforms like eBay, Amazon, or even Facebook Marketplace, where gently used timers are sold for a fraction of their original price. Discount stores also carry inexpensive visual timers, which can provide the same benefit.

Whiteboards and sticky notes are other budget-friendly tools that offer substantial organizational support. Whiteboards allow your child to see their daily schedule or reminders, which can reduce confusion and increase focus. Sticky notes can be used as visual reminders that are movable and adaptable, helping children with ADHD track tasks and mark off completed items. They also provide a sense of accomplishment when tasks are checked off.

For digital options, Trello or Microsoft To-Do are free apps that allow you to organize tasks and set reminders, providing the same visual aid as a physical board. These apps can be particularly useful for older children or those who enjoy using technology. You can use them to create lists of tasks, prioritize assignments, and track progress.

CREATIVE REPURPOSING: TOOLS FROM EVERYDAY ITEMS

Repurposing everyday household items into ADHD tools is cost-effective and a way to foster creativity and resourcefulness. This approach's benefits extend beyond saving money—it encourages problem-solving and gives children a sense of ownership over the tools they use to manage their ADHD.

For example, a simple kitchen timer can become a tool for task management. The Pomodoro Technique, developed by Francesco Cirillo, improves focus by breaking work into structured intervals and has been shown to help children with ADHD manage their focus and avoid burnout. Traditionally, it involves 25-minute work sessions (Pomodoros) followed by 5-minute breaks, with a 15–30 minute break after four cycles. However, for children, especially those with ADHD, shorter intervals work best:

- Younger children (5–7 years old): 10–15 minutes work → 5-minute break
- Older children (8–12 years old): 15–20 minutes work → 5-minute break
- Teens (13+ years old): 20–25 minutes work → 5-minute break

A good tip is to start with shorter work times (5–10 minutes) and gradually increase as focus improves. Use the kitchen timer to break homework time into these more manageable intervals, making sure to also use it for the break times!

Another budget-friendly idea is to transform old shoeboxes or storage bins into storage organizers for art supplies, school materials, or toys. A well-organized environment can help children with ADHD focus better by reducing distractions and helping them easily access the necessary tools. Organizing materials in clear bins or containers also helps children with ADHD develop organizational skills, which is essential for their overall development.

A great DIY tool is a weighted lap pad. Weighted objects are known to provide calming pressure, helping children with ADHD feel more grounded and focused. Make your lap pad by filling a fabric pouch with rice, dried beans, or stones. This weighted object can be placed on your child's lap during tasks like homework or reading, providing deep touch pressure that promotes focus and relaxation.

Finally, plastic containers, jars, or even old cereal boxes can be repurposed into sensory bins. Sensory bins are excellent for tactile stimulation and help children with ADHD focus and self-regulate. Fill a plastic container with rice, beans, or sand, and hide small objects inside. This encourages your child to dig and explore, promoting sensory integration and fine motor skills.

DIY SENSORY TOOLS AND ACTIVITIES

While repurposed sensory bins are wonderful for tactile play at home, you can also create individual tools that are more portable and accessible. Creating some sensory tools at home is an affordable and fun way to help your child manage sensory overload, regulate emotions, and improve focus. Sensory processing issues are common in children with ADHD, and having DIY sensory tools on hand can provide immediate relief when your child is overwhelmed.

Sensory bottles are an easy and calming tool. Making one is very easy, and fun too! Follow the steps below:

1. Fill a clear bottle halfway with warm water.
2. Add a couple of tablespoons of clear glue or baby oil.
3. Pour in glitter, sequins, buttons, beads, or any other small items to add visual interest. You can also experiment with adding a few drops of food coloring.
4. Secure the lid of the bottle tightly, then shake and watch the contents slowly settle.

This simple sensory tool has a calming effect and helps children refocus during transitions, particularly when feeling overwhelmed.

Homemade playdough is another sensory tool that can help with self-regulation. The tactile experience of kneading the dough provides sensory feedback that calms the nervous system. Add essential oils, like lavender or chamomile, to the dough to enhance its calming effect. Not only is this a fun activity, but it also provides a therapeutic outlet for your child's energy and emotions.

ART AND MUSIC IDEAS

Research shows that art and music therapy can be incredibly effective in helping children with ADHD by improving focus, emotional regulation, impulse control, and executive functioning. These creative activities engage the brain's reward system, increasing dopamine levels, which supports attention and self-regulation. Luckily, these creative outlets don't necessarily require professional therapists or expensive equipment—simple home materials can become powerful therapeutic tools.

To do art therapy at home, you only need basic supplies—paper, crayons, markers, or clay. The focus is on the creative process rather than creating a perfect piece of art. Drawing, painting, and sculpting allow your child to express emotions they might not have the words for, offering a calming outlet when feeling overwhelmed. Allowing your child to create freely also allows them to explore and manage their feelings without judgment. Meanwhile, activities like mandala coloring promote relaxation and patience, and more open-ended art projects allow for creative expression while reinforcing delayed gratification.

Music therapy can also be highly beneficial in improving focus and attention, and you don't need an expensive set of instruments. Instead, you can use simple household objects like tambourines, drums, or even pots and pans to create rhythm and sound. Indeed, listening to rhythmic music has been shown to help children with ADHD regulate their emotions, improve their attention span, and enhance focus, particularly during academic tasks. Meanwhile, musical training is known to strengthen brain regions responsible for attention and memory.

Alternatively, create calming playlists using free online resources like YouTube or Spotify. Many channels offer music specifically designed for relaxation and emotional regulation. These playlists can be used during homework time, bedtime routines, or when your child needs to calm down after a stressful event. Simply listening to music stimulates dopamine release, improving motivation and cognitive flexibility.

Family involvement in these creative activities can further enhance their therapeutic benefits. Consider having family painting sessions or dance parties where everyone participates. Shared art or music projects create a sense of bonding and unity while providing your child with a safe, non-verbal way to express themselves.

INSIGHTS FROM THE THERAPY ROOM

I've worked with numerous families who struggle with the financial pressures of managing ADHD. One family I worked with, the Martils, was particularly concerned about the cost of therapy and medication for their 8-year-old son, Rehan. They were already working with a speech therapist and had a behavioral plan. Still, they sought additional, cost-effective tools to complement Rehan's therapy and support his daily routine.

I recommended several DIY solutions, including using a visual timer for homework sessions and a whiteboard for daily routines. We also created a sensory toolkit for Rehan, including a sensory bottle, weighted lap pad, and DIY playdough. These tools were affordable and provided Rehan with immediate support when he became overstimulated or had difficulty transitioning between activities. The sensory bottle became a go-to tool for calming him during homework time, while the weighted lap pad helped him stay focused and grounded.

In addition, the Martils encouraged Rehan to create playlists of his favorite music and prompted him take 10 minutes to listen to music whenever he needed a "reset". They also made sure he had a space in the garage for creative projects, as this was another outlet he found helpful when becoming overwhelmed.

My experiences with this family underscored for me that ADHD management doesn't have to be financially overwhelming. With resourcefulness and the use of everyday items, families can create a supportive environment that complements therapy and helps children thrive.

KEY TAKEAWAYS

1. **ADHD support doesn't need to be expensive—** resourcefulness is your greatest asset.
2. **Visual tools like timers and whiteboards help structure routines**, smooth transitions, and reduce anxiety.
3. **DIY sensory activities foster creativity and bonding** while cost-effectively addressing sensory needs.
4. **Art and music therapy** provide valuable emotional regulation tools that can be easily incorporated into daily life.

Links to Additional Resources

- **Trello**: A free, visually organized tool for task management and scheduling. Great for ADHD. https://trello.com

- **Trello for ADHD**: Learn how to set up Trello for ADHD-related task management and visual planning. https://www.additudemag.com/trello-adhd-task-management/
- **Focus Booster**: A simple, digital timer based on the Pomodoro technique that helps break tasks into intervals. https://www.focusboosterapp.com
- **Pinterest for DIY ADHD Tools**: Search for many DIY ideas and sensory tool projects. https://www.pinterest.com
- **Additude Magazine**: A treasure trove of articles, resources, and expert advice for managing ADHD. https://www.additudemag.com

With these added resources, creative DIY strategies, and guidance, you are well-equipped to help your child with ADHD navigate daily challenges effectively and cost-efficiently.

WHAT'S NEXT?

We've covered a variety of cost-effective tools to support your child at home, but it's equally important to support your child's success at school. Let's apply this approach to helping your child thrive within the education system.

SIX
NAVIGATING THE EDUCATION SYSTEM

Stepping into your child's classroom for a parent-teacher conference can feel daunting. You're trying to focus on the teacher's words while your mind races with questions. You're eager to understand how your child is doing, but navigating the education system can sometimes feel like deciphering a complex puzzle. You've heard whispers about IEPs and 504 Plans, but what do they mean? And how can they help your child thrive?

In this chapter, we'll guide you through understanding IEPs, 504 Plans, productive school meetings, building partnerships with teachers, creating ADHD-friendly classrooms, advocating effectively, and leveraging technology to support your child's learning journey.

INDIVIDUALIZED EDUCATION PROGRAMS (IEPS) AND 504 PLANS

Individualized Education Programs (IEPs) and 504 Plans are essential tools in the U.S. education system designed to support students with disabilities, ensuring they receive the accommodations and services needed to succeed in school. While both provide support, they serve different purposes and are governed by distinct legal frameworks.

Understanding an IEP (Individualized Education Program)

An IEP is a legally binding document developed under the Individuals with Disabilities Education Act (IDEA). It is designed for students whose disabilities significantly impact their ability to learn and require specialized instruction. The process of obtaining an IEP involves a formal evaluation to determine eligibility.

Think of an IEP as a tailored suit—customized to fit the child's unique learning needs. IEPs are developed by an IEP team, which typically includes the child's parents, general and special education teachers, a school psychologist or other specialist, a school administrator, and the student (when appropriate). This team meets at least once a year to evaluate progress and adjust the IEP as needed, ensuring that the educational program remains effective and responsive to the child's needs.

Understanding a 504 Plan

A 504 Plan, on the other hand, is governed by Section 504 of the Rehabilitation Act of 1973. It is intended for students with disabilities who do not require specialized instruction but still need accommodations to access the general education curriculum on an equal basis with their peers.

A 504 Plan is more flexible than an IEP and does not require specialized instruction or as frequent progress monitoring. It is typically created by a school team that includes teachers, counselors, and administrators, and it does not require the involvement of special education staff.

Key Differences Between an Individualized Education Program (IEP) and a 504 Plan

Feature	IEP	504 Plan
Legal Basis	IDEA (Individuals with Disabilities Education Act)	Section 504 of the Rehabilitation Act of 1973
Eligibility	Student must have a disability that affects educational performance and requires specialized instruction	Student has a disability that affects learning but does not require specialized instruction
Scope	Covers specialized instruction, services, and accommodations	Covers accommodations only, no specialized instruction required
Examples of Support	Small-group instruction, speech therapy, one-on-one tutoring, behavior intervention plans	Extended time, modified seating, assistive technology, behavior plans
Review Process	Annual review with formal progress tracking	Periodic review, less formal process
Enforcement	Legally binding document, enforceable by law	Less strict legal oversight but still protects student rights

Both IEPs and 504 Plans are designed to remove barriers to learning and provide equal educational opportunities. Understanding the differences allows parents and educators to advocate effectively for students, ensuring they receive the right level of support to thrive academically and socially.

Which One Is Right for My Child?

You might still be wondering, "Which plan is right for my child?" An IEP is for children who meet specific disability categories under IDEA and require specialized instruction. A 504 Plan, on the other hand, can provide accommodations for children whose disabilities impact major life activities but not to the extent that they require modifications to the curriculum.

Real-Life Example – IEP:

Sarah's son, Ben, had ADHD and struggled with reading due to difficulties with attention and focus. After his parents collaborated with the school team, Ben was approved for an IEP, which included small-group reading support and access to text-to-speech software. Within months, Ben's reading confidence and skills improved, and he went from dreading reading assignments to finishing books for fun.

Real-Life Example – 504 Plan:

Jeremy's daughter, Jordan, had ADHD, making it difficult for her to stay seated, focus on multi-step directions, and complete assignments. While she did not require specialized instruction, her school team developed a 504 Plan to include extended time on tests, movement breaks, a quiet workspace, and teacher check-ins. These accommodations helped Jordan stay engaged and complete her work without feeling overwhelmed, allowing her to thrive academically while managing her ADHD symptoms.

PREPARING FOR PRODUCTIVE SCHOOL MEETINGS

Stepping into a school meeting without preparation is like showing up to a potluck empty-handed; it leaves you scrambling and unprepared. Thorough preparation is crucial. It ensures you walk in confidently, ready to advocate effectively for your child's needs. But where to begin?

Start by reviewing past academic reports and records, as these will reveal patterns in your child's performance and highlight areas that need attention. Take notes on any significant changes or ongoing challenges and review the reports and recommendations of any specialists that might be involved in your child's care. Finally, know what you want to achieve—whether it's discussing specific accommodations, addressing behavioral issues, or planning for your child's long-term educational goals. Clear objectives will keep discussions focused and productive.

Effective communication during these meetings is also key. Approach your child's educators with a collaborative and respectful tone and avoid coming off as confrontational. Remember - you're all part of the same team, working towards the common goal of your child's success. This means listening actively to the educators' perspectives while voicing your concerns and suggestions. Use specific, open-ended questions to gather detailed information. Instead of asking, "Is my child doing well?" try, "Can you share some examples of how my child engages with the class material?" This approach invites detailed responses, giving you a clearer picture of your child's school experience. Through a constructive dialogue, meaningful outcomes can be achieved.

Another tip is to keep detailed records of meetings and correspondence, as they serve as a reference for future discussions. Take notes during the meeting to capture key points, decisions, and any commitments made by the school. After the meeting, request written confirmation of any agreed-upon accommodations or actions. This step is crucial for accountability, ensuring everyone is on the same page and has a clear plan. Documenting these interactions creates a paper trail that can be invaluable if questions or disputes arise later, or when staff changes occur.

Following up after the meeting is just as important as the meeting itself. It's easy for plans to fall by the wayside in the hustle and bustle of daily school life. To prevent this, schedule regular check-ins with teachers to monitor your child's progress. These can be brief meetings or email updates, but they keep the lines of communication open. During these check-ins, discuss any adjustments needed to the plan. Is the current strategy working, or does it need tweaking? Ensure that agreed-upon actions are implemented and that your child's needs remain a priority. Maintaining an ongoing dialogue reinforces your role as an active participant in your child's education.

Real-Life Example: James' parents noticed he struggled with focus and task completion at school. Before their first meeting, they collected reports from his psychologist and teachers and examples of incomplete homework. Armed with this evidence, they worked collaboratively with the school to secure a 504 Plan, which included frequent movement breaks and the provision of visual checklists for assignments. Within weeks, James' focus and task completion showed dramatic improvement.

BUILDING COLLABORATIVE RELATIONSHIPS WITH TEACHERS

Picture this: you're dropping off your child at school, exchanging a quick smile and wave with their teacher. It might seem insignificant, but this small gesture is the first step towards building a collaborative relationship (as my husband, an educator, will tell you!). In fact, establishing a strong partnership with your child's teacher can profoundly impact their educational experience. When you work together, you better understand your child's needs, creating a consistent approach that bridges the gap between home and school. This consistency provides your child with a stable environment, reinforcing the strategies and support they receive and ultimately fostering their academic and social growth.

Building and maintaining these positive relationships requires intentional effort and clear communication. Start by scheduling regular communication, such as weekly email updates, to inquire about your child's progress and any challenges they might be facing. Even informal conversations, such as brief chats during pick-up and drop-off, can reveal vital information that could otherwise get 'lost' in the rush of the school term. If time allows, consider participating in school events; volunteering can strengthen your connection with the entire school community. Whether helping with a field trip or attending a classroom party, being present shows your commitment and enables you to understand the school environment better.

Approaching teachers with empathy and understanding can make a world of difference. Remember, teachers juggle various responsibilities and face their own challenges. Acknowledging their workload and the demands of managing a diverse classroom fosters goodwill and mutual respect. When you share insights into your child's strengths and preferences, you provide valuable information and show that you value the teacher's perspective and expertise. This two-way street of empathy and understanding can lead to a more effective collaboration, where both parties feel heard and respected, and your child benefits from a cohesive support system.

However, even in the most collaborative partnerships, conflicts may arise, but they don't have to derail your partnership. Addressing disagreements constructively is key to maintaining a healthy relationship. Mediation with a school counselor can be a helpful tool, providing a neutral space to discuss issues and come to a resolution. Focus on shared goals for your child's success and remember that you're both advocating for the same outcome: your child's well-being and development. By keeping the lines of communication open and approaching conflicts with a problem-solving mindset, you can navigate disagreements effectively and strengthen your partnership with the teacher.

Real-Life Example: Sophie, an 11-year-old girl with ADHD, was bright and creative but often struggled with staying focused during lessons and turning in assignments on time. Her teacher noticed she would start tasks enthusiastically but quickly become distracted, leaving many assignments unfinished. At home, her parents saw similar patterns with homework and organization, often leading to frustration for both Sophie and her family.

Determined to support her, Sophie's parents met with her teacher to discuss potential strategies. Together, they developed a personalized support plan that would help Sophie stay on track both in the classroom and at home. Her teacher introduced a color-coded planner to help her manage homework and deadlines, while also breaking assignments into smaller, more manageable tasks to prevent her from feeling overwhelmed. To provide additional structure, Sophie was paired with a check-in buddy—meeting with her teacher at the start and end of the day to review expectations and progress. Recognizing her need for movement, her teacher also incorporated short breaks between tasks to help her refocus.

With these consistent strategies in place, Sophie's confidence grew, and she began completing more assignments on time. The regular communication between her parents and teacher ensured that adjustments could be made when necessary, creating a supportive and structured environment that helped her thrive academically and socially. By working together, Sophie's parents and teacher gave her the tools she needed to succeed, reinforcing that collaboration between home and school can make a profound difference for children with ADHD.

WHAT DOES AN ADHD-FRIENDLY LEARNING ENVIRONMENT LOOK LIKE?

An ADHD-friendly classroom should be designed to support active, focused learning. The goal is to provide options that cater to individual needs, turning a traditional classroom into a dynamic learning environment. Think flexible seating arrangements, visual aids and organizational tools, simple, colorful charts, labeled bins, and calendars that serve as visual cues to help students organize their thoughts and tasks. These elements transform the classroom into a landscape where students with ADHD can thrive.

More and more teachers are regularly implementing practical strategies to better accommodate students with ADHD, such as incorporating movement breaks into the schedule. These "brain breaks" can be as simple as a quick stretch or a walk around the classroom. Students release any pent-up energy, and research supports that students' focus is improved. Multi-sensory teaching methods can be employed to engage different senses, making learning more interactive. For example, using 3D blocks in math lessons or incorporating music into language arts can make abstract concepts more tangible. These methods cater to various learning styles, ensuring students with ADHD remain engaged and motivated.

The classroom's physical environment also plays a pivotal role in supporting students with ADHD. Imagine a space where different seating options allow students to find what works best. Maybe it's a wiggle chair that lets them bounce as they focus on their tasks or a standing desk for those who find sitting still for extended periods too much of a challenge. Strategic seating arrangements can minimize distractions, placing students where they can focus. This might mean sitting them closer to the teacher or away from high-traffic areas. Meanwhile, calming colors and lighting contribute to a soothing atmosphere, reducing overstimulation. Soft hues like blues and greens and natural or dimmed lighting create a space where students can concentrate without feeling overwhelmed. These thoughtful design choices can significantly affect a student's ability to focus and learn.

This might all sound like a fantasy, but it is becoming increasingly common to find ADHD-friendly classrooms (I know I was surprised when visiting my children's new school to find beanbags, standing desks, wiggle chairs, and toned-down decorations as standard!). Even if this is not the case at your child's school, parents can still collaborate with teachers to share successful strategies used at home, for instance, a particular organizational or calming method that has worked wonders for your child. Sharing these insights can inform classroom adjustments, ensuring consistency between home and school. Parents might also consider donating or suggesting specific resources, such as fidget tools or noise-canceling headphones, which can benefit their child and the entire class. This collaborative effort fosters a community of understanding and support, where everyone works together to create an environment that meets the needs of all students.

Real-Life Example: Following discussions with his parents, Oliver's teacher implemented short "brain breaks" throughout the school day, allowing Oliver and his classmates to engage in a two-minute stretch or quick activity to reset their focus. These brief movement breaks helped Oliver release excess energy, making it easier for him to concentrate when returning to his work. In addition, his teacher introduced a laminated daily schedule, fixed to his desk, which provided a clear visual guide to keep him organized and prepared for each lesson.

The impact of these small changes was profound. With structured movement built into his day and a clear system for staying organized, Oliver became more engaged in class, started completing tasks more efficiently, and even began looking forward to participating in lessons. By working together, his parents and teacher created an environment where Oliver could thrive—proving that simple, thoughtful adjustments can make a world of difference for students with ADHD.

LEVERAGING TECHNOLOGY IN EDUCATION

Technology can be a game-changer for students with ADHD, enhancing learning and organization in ways traditional methods might not. Educational apps designed for focus and productivity can transform how your child manages tasks. Apps like Focus@Will use scientifically optimized music to boost concentration, turning study sessions into productive sprints rather than tedious marathons. Assistive technology tools further support writing and reading, offering features like text-to-speech to help decode complex passages or speech-to-text to capture ideas without the disruption of handwriting.

If your child tends to struggle with organizing their schoolwork, consider notetaking apps like Evernote, which allow students to organize their thoughts digitally, providing a structured space for class notes, reminders, and multimedia content. Apps like this help students with ADHD keep track of their assignments and thoughts, reducing the chaos that often accompanies a busy school day. Time-tracking apps are another valuable resource, helping students manage their time effectively. By setting timers for specific tasks, such as homework assignments, they can break their work into manageable chunks, reducing procrastination and increasing productivity. These digital allies can distinguish between a productive afternoon, and one spent constantly nagged at by their frustrated parents.

However, (as you probably already know), there's a fine line between using technology as a tool and letting it become a distraction. Establishing balance is essential. Screen-time guidelines help manage the allure of endless scrolling and ensure technology serves its intended purpose. Encourage tech-free zones and times, such as during meals or before bed, to create spaces where your child can unplug and engage with the world around them. Consider, for example, introducing "Technology-free Tuesday", where the whole family stays off-line after dinner and plays a board game, ping pong, or other fun activity. This balance fosters healthier habits and prevents technology from becoming a crutch, ensuring it remains a supportive tool rather than a hindrance.

Collaboration with educators is key to integrating technology effectively into your child's learning plan. Regularly share feedback on the effectiveness of the tech tools your child uses. Are they helping your child stay organized, or do they create additional distractions? Open dialogue with teachers can help tailor technology-based assignments to suit your child's unique needs. A teacher can incorporate a particular app into their lesson plan, allowing your child to use a tool they're already comfortable with in a new context. This collaboration ensures that technology enhances learning rather than complicating it, creating a seamless integration between home and school.

As we conclude this chapter, remember that technology is not a one-size-fits-all solution. It's a versatile tool that, when used thoughtfully, can bridge gaps and open doors. By leveraging the right apps and tools, you equip your child with the resources they need to thrive academically. This chapter is a steppingstone toward a more engaging and supportive educational journey for your child, guiding them toward success in the digital age.

Let's Put This into Practice: A 5-Step Parent Guide

You've read the chapter; now it's time to take action. Here's a practical 5-step guide to help you navigate the education system, advocate for your child, and build a supportive learning environment at home and school.

1. Understand IEPs & 504 Plans

Before you can advocate for your child, it's essential to understand which support plan is the right fit.

- **Know the Key Differences**:
    - An IEP is for students who require specialized instruction due to a disability affecting educational performance.
    - A 504 Plan provides accommodations to help students with disabilities succeed in a general education setting but does not include specialized instruction.
- **Gather Necessary Documentation**:
    - Collect evaluations, medical records, and teacher observations that demonstrate your child's needs.
    - If your child is struggling but does not have an official diagnosis, request an evaluation from the school.
- **Ask Questions**:
    - What specific support does my child need?
    - How will the school measure progress?

- What services are available, and how are they delivered?

Action Step:

If your child already has an IEP or 504 Plan, review it annually to ensure it still meets their needs. If they don't have one, request a meeting with the school to discuss possible supports.

2. Prepare for Productive School Meetings

School meetings can be overwhelming, but preparation is key to ensuring your child receives the support they need.

- **Review Your Child's Progress:**
    - Gather report cards, test results, teacher emails, and any behavioral reports to identify patterns in their performance.
    - Write down your concerns, questions, and goals for the meeting.
- **Communicate Clearly & Collaboratively:**
    - Approach meetings with a team mindset—you and the school share the same goal: your child's success.
    - If something isn't working, express concerns with solutions in mind. Example:
        - Instead of saying, "My child is struggling in math," try "Could we explore extra support, such as small-group instruction or additional practice materials?"
- **Document & Follow Up:**
    - Take notes during the meeting and ask for written confirmation of decisions made.

- Send a follow-up email summarizing key takeaways and next steps.

Action Step:

Before your next school meeting, write down three key concerns and one possible solution for each. Bring these to the meeting to stay focused and proactive.

3. Build Strong Partnerships with Teachers

A positive relationship with teachers ensures that everyone is working toward the same goal—your child's success.

- **Establish Open Communication**:
    - Ask teachers how they prefer to communicate (email, phone calls, or parent-teacher meetings).
    - Share insights about your child's strengths, challenges, and learning style.
- **Be Involved in School Life**:
    - Attend parent-teacher conferences, workshops, and school events to stay engaged.
    - Volunteer when possible—it strengthens relationships and gives insight into the school environment.
- **Address Concerns Constructively**:
    - If an issue arises, approach it calmly and with problem-solving in mind.
    - Example: Instead of saying, "You're not supporting my child enough," try "I've noticed my child is struggling with transitions. What strategies can we try to help them stay focused?"

Action Step:

Email or call your child's teacher this week to check in on progress and ask how you can support learning at home.

4. Leverage Technology Thoughtfully

Technology can be a powerful tool for children with ADHD, learning disabilities, or executive function challenges—if used strategically.

- **Use Tools for Focus & Organization**:
    - Audiobooks or text-to-speech software for reading support
    - Pomodoro timers or visual schedules for task management
    - Digital planners or apps like Google Calendar or Trello for organization
- **Introduce Assistive Learning Tools**:
    - Speech-to-text software for kids who struggle with writing
    - Noise-canceling headphones to reduce distractions
    - Math apps with step-by-step explanations for difficult concepts
- **Create a Healthy Balance**:
    - Set screen-time limits and encourage breaks using timers.
    - Work with teachers to align digital tools with classroom strategies.

Action Step:

Try one new assistive technology tool this week to support your child's learning—whether it's a timer for focus, an audiobook for reading, or an app for organization.

CHAPTER REFLECTION

Navigating the education system may feel daunting, but you are not alone. This chapter's tools, strategies, and stories show that preparation, advocacy, and collaboration make meaningful progress possible. Each step you take makes a difference, empowering your child to thrive both in the classroom and beyond. Remember, you are your child's greatest advocate and ally.

KEY TAKEAWAYS

- **IEP vs 504 Plans**: IEPs provide specialized instruction, while 504 Plans focus on accommodations in general education.
- **Success is the celebration of preparation**: Thorough preparation and clear objectives are key to productive school meetings.
- **Connect before you correct**: Strong parent-teacher relationships create a supportive and consistent environment for your child and lay the foundation for constructive conversations.
- **Be flexible**: ADHD-friendly classrooms use flexible seating, movement breaks, and visual aids to maximize learning.

- **Technology - friend or foe**: When used thoughtfully and in balance, technology can enhance organization, focus, and learning. However, clear limits need to be set.

WHAT'S NEXT?

Support doesn't stop at school. Let's explore the broader community resources that can bolster your efforts and enrich your child's experience.

SEVEN
COMMUNITY AND SUPPORT NETWORKS

I magine standing in a crowded room, unsure where to start or who to talk to, with the weight of your child's ADHD struggles feeling like a heavy backpack that only you can see. It's a feeling many parents know all too well—a sense of isolation amid a crowd. What if you could find a small group within that crowd, parents just like you, each carrying their own invisible backpacks filled with stories, challenges, and insights? With each conversation, shared understanding and empathy deepen. Strategies emerge naturally—from managing impulsive behaviors to finding the best local therapist—illuminating paths you might otherwise not have considered. These shared moments, big and small, reveal the true strength of the community.

In this chapter, we explore how building and maintaining strong support networks can transform the challenges of parenting a child with ADHD into opportunities for connection, growth, and shared wisdom.

FINDING SUPPORT NETWORKS

Knowing where to look is the first step in building a strong support network. Local parenting groups are often an invaluable resource, offering regular meetups and workshops tailored to parents of children with ADHD. These groups might meet in community centers or even local coffee shops, providing a relaxed environment where you can connect with others who understand the challenges of ADHD parenting. ADHD-specific events, such as family fun days or seminars, are also excellent opportunities to meet like-minded individuals. These events offer a chance for practical advice and a sense of belonging, reminding you that you're not navigating this journey alone.

Being part of a support network means connecting with people from diverse backgrounds and experiences. Parents of older children or teenagers with ADHD often have valuable insights to share, as they've already navigated many of the challenges you may be facing. Their experiences can offer hope and reassurance, showing you that overcoming difficult moments and emerging stronger is possible. Additionally, connecting with parents from different cultural backgrounds broadens your perspective and introduces new strategies you might not have considered whether it's structured study habits, alternative discipline techniques, or different approaches to advocacy. Insights from different cultural perspectives can help create a more supportive and inclusive learning environment for your child.

While finding these networks takes some time, it is achievable. Meanwhile, maintaining these connections requires some commitment. Attending regular meetups or casual coffee mornings helps reinforce the relationships you've built. These gatherings provide a touchpoint for checking in, offering support, and sharing advice. Digital platforms such as group chats or online forums can serve as an additional lifeline, allowing you to reach out for advice or a listening ear on difficult days. These ongoing connections create a sense of continuity and ensure that help is always available when you need it.

PRACTICAL RESOURCES FOR PARENTS

There is an abundance of resources available to parents of children with ADHD, ranging from online communities to local support networks. These resources can provide vital information, tools, and support, helping you navigate the complexities of ADHD parenting.

Facebook support groups, such as "ADHD Parent Support Group," "Parenting ADHD and Autism," and "Moms with ADHD," are widespread platforms where parents share their experiences, offer advice, and connect with others who truly understand their struggles. These groups provide a safe space for discussing various aspects of ADHD, from behavior management strategies to finding professional help.

Websites like Understood.org, CHADD (Children and Adults with Attention-Deficit/Hyperactivity Disorder), and ADDitude Magazine are excellent sources of information. They offer articles, expert guidance, and resources to help you better understand ADHD and how to support your child. These sites are often updated with the latest research and tips for managing ADHD at home, in school, and within the community.

Many community centers and local libraries host parenting workshops and ADHD-specific events. These can provide in-person support and offer the chance to connect with local parents facing similar challenges. Schools and healthcare providers are also excellent starting points for finding local support groups or resources, as they often host workshops or can refer you to trusted services.

In addition to online resources and community groups, there are helpful apps for ADHD management. Apps like "Brain Focus" help children and parents stay focused with timed work and rest intervals. At the same time, "Headspace" offers mindfulness and meditation exercises to reduce stress, which is especially beneficial for overwhelmed parents.

Interactive Element: Creating Your Support Network

Take a moment to think about potential resources and support groups in your community. Start by researching local ADHD-specific meetups or parenting groups. You could also explore online forums and social media groups for advice and connection. Try reaching out to at least one new group or individual this week, whether attending a local event, joining an online forum, or simply sending a message to a fellow parent you've met. By making small efforts to connect, you'll build a meaningful support network that can offer practical guidance and emotional support.

SHARING STORIES: CREATING A COMMUNITY OF EMPATHY

There's a unique comfort in sitting across from someone who truly understands—another parent who has walked the same path, faced the same challenges, and felt the same frustrations and triumphs. As you recount the latest episode of your child hiding under the table at a family gathering, a knowing smile or a reassuring nod reminds you that you are not alone. Shared moments of vulnerability offer both relief and reassurance. In a world that often feels isolating, storytelling becomes a bridge, creating a community where empathy, understanding, and support can flourish.

Consider hosting informal storytelling circles where parents can gather to share their experiences. The narratives shared in these spaces often mirror your own experiences, highlighting the common threads that unite you. Whether it's a tip on managing homework battles or a suggestion for establishing a morning routine that works, these stories carry practical wisdom from those who've walked the same path.

Additionally, online platforms such as community newsletters or social media groups can offer a broader space for storytelling. These digital spaces allow you to share your experiences with a wider audience, reaching parents who may not have local support but still long for connection. The benefits of vulnerability and sharing your journey cannot be overstated. It strengthens the community and allows for personal healing and growth.

INSIGHTS FROM THE THERAPY ROOM

I often work with families who feel isolated and overwhelmed by the challenges of raising a child with ADHD. One family came to me after struggling for months to manage their 12-year-old daughter Amara's behavior. Amara tended to act impulsively, struggle with focus, and often got into conflicts with her younger siblings, which left her parents feeling drained and unsure of where to turn.

I encouraged Ravi and Aisha, Amara's parents, to join a local support group for parents of children with ADHD. At first, they were hesitant, feeling that their problems were too unique or personal to share. However, after attending a few meetings, Ravi and Aisha began to open up, realizing that many other parents were facing similar challenges. One parent shared how they had worked through sibling conflicts by setting up a joint "chore chart" to give the children more structure and reduce competition for attention.

Another parent shared their experience creating quiet time family rituals, which helped minimize overstimulation and impulsivity.

These shared stories provided Ravi and Aisha with both practical strategies and emotional comfort. They felt less alone on their parenting journey and began to feel more empowered, knowing they had a community of people who understood and supported them. Over time, they implemented some of the strategies discussed in the group, such as creating a routine for Amara that included regular breaks, clear expectations, and lots of positive reinforcement. As a result, Amara's behavior improved, while Ravi and Aisha felt more confident in their ability to handle challenges.

This experience underscored the profound impact that community support can have on parents of children with ADHD, a safe space where parents can share advice, find comfort, build resilience, and gain the confidence they need to thrive.

Reflection Section: Share Your Story

Take a moment to reflect on a recent challenge or success with your child. Write it down, focusing on the emotions and lessons learned. Consider sharing this story with friends, community groups, or online forums. Your story might be the key to understanding and empathy for someone else. By sharing your experiences, you contribute to a supportive, open community that helps everyone involved grow stronger.

Actionable Steps: 8-Step Guide to Build and Strengthen Support Networks

1. **Identify Local Resources**: Research community centers, libraries, schools, or healthcare providers for parenting groups or ADHD-focused events. Create a list of 5 local (or virtual) gatherings you can join.
2. **Explore Online Platforms**: Join reputable Facebook groups, Slack, or Discord communities tailored to ADHD support.
3. **Attend Regular Meetups**: Commit to attending local or virtual gatherings to establish and maintain connections with other parents at least once a month.
4. **Leverage Practical Tools**: Download and use apps like Brain Focus and Headspace to manage ADHD and relieve parental stress.
5. **Seek Mentorship**: Consider contacting experienced parents or professionals for more one-on-one advice and guidance.
6. **Share and Listen**: Commit to being active in your community by sharing your experiences and learning from others' stories.
7. **Review Strategies Regularly**: Periodically evaluate what resources and strategies are working and adapt as necessary.
8. **Prioritize Self-Care**: Don't forget to engage in activities that recharge you so you can bring your best self to your parenting journey.

KEY TAKEAWAYS

- **Building a support network transforms isolation into connection**, offering emotional and practical benefits.
- **Use resources**, from local community events to online platforms, to strengthen your network.
- **Sharing your story fosters empathy, trust, and deeper community bonds**.
- **Prioritizing self-care** enhances your ability to engage with and benefit from support systems.
- **Taking small, actionable steps** builds a sustainable and effective support network.

By connecting with others and sharing experiences, you create a community of support and understanding, helping you navigate the challenges of parenting a child with ADHD with greater strength and resilience.

WHAT'S NEXT?

After building a support network, the final step is to plan for your child's future and help them transition confidently into adulthood.

EIGHT
PLANNING FOR THE FUTURE

Adolescence is a transformative period for all children, but it presents unique challenges and opportunities for children with ADHD. This chapter explores adolescence's physical, emotional, and social changes while providing strategies to support independence, confidence, and resilience in your child.

Childhood is a daunting time for many young people. Leaving behind the comfort of childhood can bring a whirlwind of hormones, emotions, and social dynamics. For children with ADHD, this developmental stage can feel even more intense, with impulsivity, emotional shifts, and social challenges amplifying the changes.

This chapter will help you navigate this transformative stage by providing practical strategies to support your child as they explore their identity, take on more responsibility, and build the skills they'll need to thrive into adulthood.

UNDERSTANDING THE CHALLENGES OF ADOLESCENCE

Adolescence is marked by a quest for self-identity. As your child begins to ask, "Who am I?" and "Where do I fit in?" they might struggle to reconcile their ADHD traits with the societal expectations around them. They may start to see themselves differently, which can be challenging, especially when they're already managing the complexities of ADHD.

Adolescents are naturally drawn to taking risks as they seek new experiences and test boundaries. This period characterizes a greater desire for independence, yet children with ADHD often face challenges with impulsiveness and self-regulation. It's essential to approach this stage with empathy and a deep understanding of their need for both guidance and space to explore.

NAVIGATING HORMONAL CHANGES AND EMOTIONAL SHIFTS

As puberty approaches, hormonal fluctuations significantly impact mood, impulse control, and emotional stability. For children with ADHD, these fluctuations may be more pronounced due to underlying challenges with emotional regulation and executive functioning. Research indicates that dopamine imbalances—already characteristic of ADHD—can interact with pubertal hormone shifts, leading to heightened mood swings, irritability, and impulsivity.

The Science Behind Emotional Shifts in Puberty and ADHD

During puberty, several key hormonal changes influence mood and behavior:

- Increased Testosterone and Estrogen:
    - Both testosterone (in boys and girls) and estrogen (more prominent in girls) impact neurotransmitter activity, including dopamine and serotonin levels, which are already dysregulated in ADHD.
    - Sudden increases can exaggerate emotional highs and lows, making children more prone to frustration, irritability, and emotional outbursts.
- Fluctuating Cortisol Levels:
    - Cortisol, the stress hormone, becomes more reactive during puberty, making emotional responses to minor stressors (like a forgotten homework assignment) more intense.
    - Children with ADHD often have difficulty moderating cortisol responses, leading to

prolonged emotional distress after an upsetting event.
- Delayed Prefrontal Cortex Maturation:
  - The prefrontal cortex, responsible for emotional regulation, impulse control, and decision-making, develops later in children with ADHD, contributing to difficulty managing mood fluctuations and social interactions.
  - This lag in development means children with ADHD may have more extreme emotional responses to everyday stressors than their neurotypical peers.
- Dopamine Dysregulation:
  - Since dopamine plays a crucial role in motivation, pleasure, and emotional balance, its irregular production in children with ADHD makes mood shifts more intense and unpredictable.
  - This can result in heightened frustration, difficulty recovering from setbacks, and emotional volatility.

How This Manifests in Daily Life

You may notice that your child:

- Overreacts to minor conflicts, such as a sibling borrowing a favorite shirt or a change in routine.
- Experiences sudden frustration or emotional shutdowns, even in non-stressful situations.
- Struggles with rejection sensitivity dysphoria (RSD) —a phenomenon common in ADHD where perceived criticism or failure feels overwhelming.

- Feels intense embarrassment or self-consciousness, especially in social situations.

HOW TO SUPPORT YOUR CHILD'S EMOTIONAL REGULATION

Understanding that hormonal changes amplify emotional responses can help parents respond with empathy rather than frustration. Here are some evidence-based strategies to help your child manage these shifts constructively:

1. **Validate and Normalize Their Experience**
   - Acknowledge their feelings without dismissing them. Instead of saying, "You're overreacting," try:
     - "I know this feels really upsetting right now. It's okay to feel frustrated. Let's figure out how we can work through this together."
   - Remind them that puberty affects emotional stability for everyone, not just those with ADHD.
2. **Implement Emotional Regulation Techniques** (discussed in previous chapters)
   - Mindfulness and Deep Breathing: Help regulate cortisol levels and reduce impulsive reactions.
   - Journaling or Emotional Mapping: Writing down emotions can provide clarity and reduce emotional overwhelm.
   - Cognitive Reframing: Teach them to challenge negative thoughts by asking, "What's another way to see this situation?"
3. **Encourage Physical Activity for Dopamine Regulation**
   - Exercise is one of the most effective natural dopamine boosters. Actively support your child

to find an activity or sport that they enjoy and encourage them to do it regularly. This might include:
- Cardiovascular exercises (running, swimming, biking)
- Strength training (lifting weights, resistance bands)
- Yoga or martial arts (both improve impulse control and emotional balance)

- Even a short walk after school can significantly improve mood and reduce frustration sensitivity.

4. **Create Predictable Routines to Promote Sleep and Downtime**
   - Maintain consistent morning and bedtime routines to ensure your child is obtaining sufficient sleep (8–10 hours)—Hormonal changes make ADHD-related sleep challenges worse. A sleep-hygiene routine (e.g., no screens before bed, calming activities) is essential.
   - Scheduled downtime—Overstimulation can lead to emotional exhaustion. Build in quiet time for reading, drawing, or listening to music.

SUPPORTING INDEPENDENCE AND RESPONSIBILITY

As children grow, increasing their responsibilities is essential for developing life skills, confidence, and self-sufficiency. In fact, research suggests that children who take on age-appropriate responsibilities develop better executive functioning skills, including planning, organization, and problem-solving. This is particularly important for children with ADHD, who often struggle with impulse control and task management due to differences in brain development, particularly in the prefrontal cortex.

Encouraging responsibility can take many forms, such as:

- Managing a school project independently
- Preparing a family meal from start to finish
- Completing household chores with minimal reminders

However, independence is not just about giving children freedom—it requires structured support to help them develop the skills to make thoughtful choices. Studies show that children with ADHD benefit from structured routines that provide clear expectations and reduce their mental load. For example, setting a specific time each day for homework, chores, or self-care helps build predictability and reduces forgetfulness.

Another effective strategy is involving children in planning and decision-making. Research in developmental psychology indicates that when children participate in setting their own goals and routines, they are more likely to follow through because they feel a sense of ownership. Encouraging them to plan their tasks, use checklists, or break large tasks into smaller steps reinforces their ability to manage responsibilities in a structured way. There are thousands of free online resources that you can use as a starting point.

Celebrating successes—both big and small—is also essential. Studies on positive reinforcement show that acknowledging a child's efforts boosts motivation and self-efficacy, reinforcing the idea that responsibility is both rewarding and empowering. Even small achievements, such as remembering to complete a chore without a reminder, can be praised to encourage consistency.

By gradually increasing responsibilities while providing structured support, children with ADHD can develop the skills they need to navigate adulthood with confidence and independence.

HELPING YOUR CHILD MANAGE RISK-TAKING BEHAVIORS

Adolescence is a period of exploration, independence, and increased risk-taking behaviors. While this is a natural part of growing up, for children with ADHD, impulsivity, thrill-seeking tendencies, and difficulty assessing long-term consequences can make risk-taking more frequent and potentially hazardous. As a parent, your role is to guide your child toward healthy, constructive risk-taking while minimizing dangerous behaviors.

Why Risk-Taking Happens

Risk-taking in adolescence is driven by biological, cognitive, and social factors.

- Brain Development and Impulse Control: The prefrontal cortex, responsible for decision-making and impulse control, develops more slowly in children with ADHD. Meanwhile, the limbic system, which drives reward-seeking behaviors, is more active during adolescence, leading to increased thrill-seeking and reduced ability to weigh risks versus

rewards. This imbalance can make high-risk behaviors feel exciting and rewarding, while potential negative consequences seem distant or unimportant.
- Dopamine and the Need for Stimulation: Children with ADHD often have lower baseline dopamine levels, making them more likely to seek out high-stimulation activities that provide an instant reward. This can lead to more impulsive decisions, such as reckless driving, experimenting with substances, engaging in risky social behaviors, or breaking rules without considering the consequences.
- Peer Influence and Social Pressure: Adolescents, especially those with ADHD, may struggle with impulse control in social situations where risk-taking is encouraged. The desire for peer acceptance can lead them to engage in risky behaviors without fully processing the long-term consequences.

What Parents Can Do

Managing risk-taking behaviors in children with ADHD requires a balance of structure, trust, and open communication. Understanding the underlying causes can help parents approach risk-taking behaviors with guidance and support, rather than frustration or punishment alone.

1. Encourage Healthy Risk-Taking

Risk-taking is not inherently bad—it can be a valuable tool for learning, growth, and confidence-building when channeled correctly. Encourage positive, structured risks that satisfy your child's need for novelty and challenge, such as:

- Trying a new sport or physical activity, such as rock climbing, mountain biking, skateboarding, or martial arts
- Taking leadership roles in clubs, debate teams, or student council
- Exploring adventurous but supervised activities, such as outdoor survival camps, coding competitions, or theater performances
- Pursuing a creative risk, such as starting a YouTube channel or performing at a talent show

By providing exciting yet safe alternatives, your child can experience the thrill of risk-taking in a constructive way.

2. Encourage Open and Honest Communication

Your child needs to feel safe talking to you about their impulses and the risks they are considering. Creating an open, judgment-free space encourages them to seek your guidance rather than hiding risky behaviors.

- Avoid overly harsh punishment for mistakes, as this may lead them to become more secretive.
- Ask open-ended questions to encourage self-reflection:
  - What makes this activity exciting for you?
  - What do you think could go wrong?
  - How would you feel if your best friend were in this situation?
- Be proactive in discussing peer pressure—do not wait for a situation to arise before addressing it.

Action Step: Have a casual conversation about a risky scenario they might encounter, such as being pressured to try vaping at a party and discuss how they might handle it.

3. Role-Play Scenarios to Build Confidence

Children with ADHD often struggle with thinking ahead in high-pressure situations. Practicing responses before they are needed helps prepare them for real-life decision-making.

- Teach refusal skills for peer pressure situations:
    - "No thanks, I'm good."
    - "I'm not into that, but you do you."
    - "I don't want to get caught and ruin my chances of [insert goal]."
- Practice problem-solving strategies:
    - If they are stuck in a risky situation, how can they exit safely?
    - Who can they call for help?
- Develop a "code word" system where they can text you discreetly if they need to be picked up from an unsafe situation.

4. Set Clear and Consistent Boundaries

Boundaries provide a sense of security and predictability, which children with ADHD often need to regulate their behavior. However, these boundaries should be discussed collaboratively rather than imposed harshly.

- Make expectations clear and enforceable:
    - "I trust you to go out with your friends, but I need

to know where you'll be and when you'll be home."
  - "If you're running late, call me instead of sneaking in. I won't be mad if you communicate."
- Explain the reasoning behind rules to increase buy-in:
  - Instead of just saying, "No drinking," explain how alcohol affects impulse control and decision-making in people with ADHD.
- Be consistent with consequences— inconsistent discipline can lead to boundary-pushing behaviors.

Action Step: Have a family meeting to discuss rules with input from your child. When kids help set boundaries, they are more likely to respect them.

5. Model Healthy Risk-Taking and Self-Control

Children with ADHD often learn best by observing rather than being told what to do. Demonstrate healthy decision-making and risk-taking strategies in your own life.

- Show them how you assess risks in your own decisions:
  - "I was nervous about speaking at work today, but I prepared and took the risk anyway."
  - "I wanted to drive faster because I was running late, but I reminded myself that staying safe is more important."
- Let them see you manage stress without impulsivity, such as taking a break instead of reacting angrily.
- Share stories of your own mistakes—help them see

that making a bad decision is not the end of the world, but learning from it matters.

EMPOWERING SELF-ADVOCACY

Self-advocacy is a vital skill for children with ADHD as they move through adolescence. Encouraging your child to speak up for themselves—whether with teachers, friends, or family members—helps them feel empowered and in control of their environment.

Start by role-playing scenarios where your child practices advocating for themselves. For example, practicing asking for extended time on assignments or requesting help when needed can help your child feel more confident in those situations. Encouraging your child to speak openly with their teachers about their challenges due to ADHD will also help them get the accommodations they need to succeed in school.

Involving your child in decisions related to their healthcare, such as communicating with their doctors or therapists, also empowers them. This is an essential part of building their ability to advocate for their needs as they age.

CAREER PLANNING AND VOCATIONAL SKILLS DEVELOPMENT

As children with ADHD approach adulthood, career planning becomes an essential step in preparing for their future. Research suggests that early career exploration and hands-on work experience help young adults with ADHD build confidence, improve executive functioning, and develop the skills needed for long-term success. Since individuals with

ADHD often thrive in stimulating, hands-on, and dynamic environments, it is important to help them explore careers that align with their interests, strengths, and working styles.

Exploring Interests and Career Pathways

Career planning should begin with exposure to different fields and experiences to help children discover their passions and talents. Research shows that individuals with ADHD often excel in creative, entrepreneurial, and fast-paced roles where problem-solving and adaptability are valued.

Strategies for career exploration include:

- Encouraging job shadowing to observe professionals in different careers
- Providing opportunities for hands-on learning through projects or hobbies
- Discussing careers that align with their natural strengths and interests

Gaining Real-World Experience

Internships, volunteer work, and part-time jobs provide valuable exposure to work environments, social skills development, and a sense of responsibility. Studies indicate that real-world experience helps ADHD individuals strengthen executive functioning skills such as time management, organization, and teamwork.

Encourage your child to:

- Volunteer in community organizations to develop teamwork and responsibility
- Participate in school leadership roles to build confidence and communication skills
- Pursue internships in areas of interest to gain career-related experience

Online Career Exploration Tools

Several online resources can help young adults explore careers based on their interests, strengths, and preferred work environments.

1. **MyNextMove** – www.mynextmove.org

MyNextMove is a **career exploration tool** that helps users identify career paths based on **skills, personality traits, and work preferences**. It offers interactive assessments and provides insights into job expectations, salary ranges, and future job growth.

2. **O*Net Online** – www.onetonline.org

O*Net Online is a **comprehensive database of occupations**, offering detailed descriptions of job responsibilities, required skills, and workplace conditions. It is particularly useful for individuals who want to explore **job demands, skill requirements, and career pathways**.

Matching Careers with Strengths and Interests

Encourage your child to consider:

- What tasks and activities energize them? (e.g., problem-solving, hands-on work, helping others)
- What environments suit their strengths? (e.g., structured vs. flexible, independent vs. team-based)
- What careers allow them to focus on their talents? (e.g., creativity, technology, healthcare, trades)

Helping young adults with ADHD identify careers that align with their strengths and natural abilities increases the likelihood of long-term job satisfaction and success. By using structured career tools, real-world experiences, and self-reflection, they can confidently navigate the transition into adulthood and the workforce.

INSIGHTS FROM THE THERAPY ROOM

As a clinical psychologist, I've worked with many adolescents with ADHD who are preparing for the future. One memorable case was with a 14-year-old named Noah, whose parents were concerned about his impulsive behaviors and how these might affect his future.

Noah's impulsiveness often led him to make decisions without considering the consequences. For instance, he'd agree to plans with friends without discussing them with his parents, sometimes getting him into trouble. His parents were frustrated, but they were also eager to help him make better decisions.

We focused on helping Noah develop his self-advocacy skills. He practiced speaking up about what he needed in school and in social situations. We also worked on helping him identify his strengths, which gave him more confidence in handling responsibility. In addition to practicing role-playing scenarios, we set up a weekly routine that helped him manage his time better, giving him a sense of control over his responsibilities.

Noah's parents also learned to communicate with him more effectively. They set clear boundaries while offering him choices, empowering him to take ownership of his decisions. Over time, Noah became more self-aware and began making decisions more thoughtfully. After careful consideration, the family moved Noah to a learning environment that was better tailored to his needs. His school grades improved, and his confidence in handling social situations grew. He discovered a love for mechanics and could see a career path ahead of him.

The process wasn't easy, but with ongoing support, Noah and his parents learned how to work together to prepare for his future. It reinforced for me that while adolescence presents challenges, it's also an opportunity to equip children with ADHD with the tools they need for independence, self-advocacy, and a bright future.

CHAPTER REFLECTION

Adolescence is a pivotal stage in your child's life, filled with emotional, physical, and social changes. As a parent of a child with ADHD, I know that navigating this time can feel overwhelming. However, by committing to open communication, teaching independence, and guiding your child through the challenges of adolescence, you are helping them develop essential life skills that will serve them well into adulthood.

Remember that this journey is not about perfection but progress. Every step, from building self-advocacy to managing risky behaviors, is essential to your child's growth. By offering consistent support, empathy, and encouragement, you create a safe space for your child to explore, learn, and mature confidently.

As you work through the strategies shared in this chapter, take pride in the small successes—whether your child speaks up for themselves, takes on new responsibilities, or handles a challenging social situation with grace. These moments of progress will build upon one another, shaping your child into a resilient, self-assured young adult.

The road ahead may not always be smooth, but with your guidance, your child will be better prepared to navigate the complexities of adolescence and step confidently into the future. Embrace this time with patience, flexibility, and a focus on the growth and opportunities ahead.

KEY TAKEAWAYS

1. **Adolescence is a time of profound change—** understanding these changes helps you support your child effectively.
    - Hormonal fluctuations, brain development, and social pressures all contribute to emotional intensity and impulsive decision-making. Recognizing these developmental shifts allows

you to respond with patience and guidance, rather than frustration.
2. **Open communication fosters trust** and provides a safe space for your child to navigate challenges.
    - Adolescents with ADHD may struggle with emotional regulation and impulsivity, making open and nonjudgmental conversations essential. Encouraging your child to express their thoughts and feelings helps them build self-awareness and problem-solving skills.
3. **Promoting independence and self-advocacy** equips your child with the tools to thrive in adulthood.
    - Teaching your child how to set goals, manage responsibilities, and advocate for themselves builds confidence and prepares them for future challenges. Allowing structured opportunities for independence—such as handling chores, managing schoolwork, or making decisions—helps develop executive functioning skills.
4. **Structured routines, self-assessment tools, and role-playing exercises** provide practical ways to build essential skills.
    - Consistent routines reduce disorganization and impulsivity, creating a predictable environment where your child can succeed. Self-assessment tools help them track their own progress, while role-playing scenarios reinforce decision-making strategies, especially in high-pressure situations like peer interactions or managing responsibilities.

5. **Career exploration and vocational skills development** help prepare your child for a successful future.
    - Exposing your child to different career options, internships, and volunteer opportunities allows them to discover strengths and interests. Utilizing online tools like MyNextMove and O*Net Online provides structured career guidance tailored to their abilities.

By embracing these strategies, you can guide your child through adolescence with confidence, helping them develop resilience, self-sufficiency, and emotional stability as they transition into adulthood. With the right support and encouragement, your child can grow into an independent, capable, and fulfilled individual.

Additional Resources

To further support your child's growth, explore these valuable tools and resources:

- Career Exploration:
    - MyNextMove – Interactive career assessment and job exploration tool.
    - O*Net Online – Comprehensive career database with skills assessments.
- Emotional and Mental Well-being:
    - Headspace – Guided meditation and mindfulness for stress management.
    - Calm – Relaxation and sleep support through mindfulness techniques.

- Organization and Productivity Tools:
  - Trello – Task management and organization tool for tracking responsibilities.
- ADHD-Specific Support:
  - Understood.org – A hub for parents and educators with expert ADHD resources.

CONCLUSION AND TAKEAWAYS

As we come to the end of this journey together, take a moment to reflect on all that you've learned. This book was intended as a guide to help you navigate the complexities of parenting a child with ADHD. Chapter 1 began with the foundational knowledge of ADHD, laying out its symptoms and impact. Providing you with this understanding was essential as it provided the foundation upon which empathy and connection could be built. Recognizing ADHD as a different way of experiencing the world, you learned the importance of open communication with your child, establishing the vital relationship that supports effective parenting.

In Chapters 2 to 4, you explored the practical aspects of daily life, discovering strategies to navigate morning routines, bedtime battles, and homework struggles with confidence and calm. These tools were complemented by a deeper dive into emotional regulation, where you uncovered methods to support your child's mental well-being and help them manage emotional outbursts effectively. Together, these approaches form a robust framework for handling the everyday challenges that come with parenting a child with ADHD.

Chapter 5 then turned to resources, offering cost-effective tools and strategies to implement these practices without straining your budget. Practicality and sustainability are key to long-term success, and this step ensured you had access to the support necessary to continue thriving. With these resources, the book guided you through the education system in Chapter 6, empowering you to collaborate with educators, secure accommodations, and advocate for your child's academic success.

Community and support networks were the focus of Chapter 7, highlighting the importance of building connections outside your immediate family. From local groups to online communities, these networks provide invaluable strength and shared experiences. They remind you that you are not alone on this journey, reinforcing the importance of seeking help and supporting others.

Finally, in Chapter 8, the book looks toward the future, preparing you and your child for adolescence and the transition into adulthood. This chapter emphasized developing independence and self-advocacy, equipping your child with the tools to approach the world confidently. The lessons on planning, building resilience, and encouraging self-reliance culminated in a hopeful vision for what lies ahead.

Parenting a child with ADHD is an ever-evolving journey of growth, learning, and love. Every step you take, no matter how small, makes a difference. Embrace the wins and learn from the challenges, knowing that your dedication is shaping a brighter future for your child. However, it is also important to remember that challenges will always exist, and there is no such thing as a perfect parent. Treat yourself with compassion as you fail, learn, and grow. Parenting is as much about your development as it is about your child's. Acknowledging your humanity allows you to parent from a place of kindness and resilience.

This book has added to your toolbox of parenting skills, but the journey doesn't end here. Keep seeking knowledge, connecting with others, and believing in your ability to guide your child toward their fullest potential. As you move forward, carry the core message of this book: understanding, empathy, and action create a foundation for success. You've got this, and your child is lucky to have you by their side. Thank you for allowing this book to be part of your parenting journey. Here's to a future filled with hope, growth, and resilience.

But wait! There is more… I wanted to offer you even more tools and information to continue your learning. Therefore, I have included three Bonus Chapters that cover what to expect during an ADHD assessment, how to explain ADHD to your child, and what treatment options are available for the effective management of ADHD symptoms. Finally, I have included a mindfulness and self-compassion-based curriculum that you and your children can work through at home as a family. The curriculum is based on my own research into the efficacy of mindfulness and self-compassion, which highlighted the importance of both parent and child working together to build these life-changing skills. Enjoy!

Bonus Content

- ADHD Assessment - What to Expect
- Explaining ADHD to Your Child
- Exploring Effective, Evidence-Based Therapy Options for Your Child with ADHD
- A Fun, Family-Focused Mindfulness and Self-Compassion Curriculum

BONUS CONTENT

ADHD ASSESSMENT – WHAT TO EXPECT

Navigating an ADHD assessment can feel overwhelming, but understanding the process can help you prepare, reduce anxiety, and advocate effectively for your child. This chapter outlines the steps involved in an ADHD evaluation, with specific details for the United States, Australia, and the United Kingdom. It also includes links to trusted online resources to provide up-to-date information and support.

PREPARING FOR THE ASSESSMENT

Before scheduling an appointment, it's essential to gather key information that will help clinicians make an accurate diagnosis.

What to Bring to the Assessment:

1. Developmental History
   - Record major milestones (e.g., walking, talking, toilet training).
   - Note any early signs of inattention, hyperactivity, or impulsivity.
2. School Records
   - Report cards, teacher feedback, and standardized test results.
   - Copies of Individualized Education Programs (IEPs), 504 Plans, or other learning support documents.
3. Behavioral Observations
   - Track specific behavioral patterns at home and in social settings.
   - Note when and where challenges occur (e.g., difficulty following instructions, excessive fidgeting, impulsive decision-making).
4. Medical History
   - List any medications, previous diagnoses, and significant health issues.
   - Include any family history of ADHD, anxiety, depression, or other mental health conditions, as ADHD is often genetic.

THE ADHD EVALUATION PROCESS

An ADHD assessment is comprehensive and typically involves multiple steps. Expect a combination of interviews, standardized tests, observations, and questionnaires to rule out other conditions and ensure an accurate diagnosis.

Step 1: Initial Intake and History Gathering

The process often begins with an initial consultation, where the clinician:

- Discusses your child's developmental, academic, and social history.
- Asks about specific concerns and reasons for seeking an evaluation.
- Reviews family history, as ADHD has a strong genetic component.

Step 2: Questionnaires and Screening Tools

Parents, teachers, and sometimes the child complete standardized ADHD rating scales to assess symptoms and behavior. These tools compare your child's behavior to developmental norms.

Common ADHD screening tools include:

- **Conners' Rating Scales** – Measures hyperactivity, impulsivity, emotional regulation, and social difficulties.
- **Vanderbilt Assessment Scales** – Evaluates ADHD symptoms alongside co-occurring issues like anxiety or learning disorders.
- **Behavior Assessment System for Children (BASC)** – Assesses behavioral and emotional functioning in children.

Step 3: Direct Observation and Clinical Interviews

A clinician may observe the child in different settings (e.g., home, school, or clinic) to assess:

- Attention span
- Impulse control
- Social interactions
- Task completion and organization

Structured clinical interviews allow the psychologist or psychiatrist to gather additional details and rule out other conditions.

Step 4: Psychological and Educational Testing

Additional tests may be recommended to evaluate cognitive abilities and learning challenges.

- Wechsler Intelligence Scale for Children (WISC-V) – Assesses general intellectual abilities and processing speed.
- Wechsler Individual Achievement Test (WIAT-III) – Measures reading, writing, and math skills to identify potential learning disabilities.
- Test of Everyday Attention for Children (TEA-Ch) – Examines sustained and selective attention.

Step 5: Ruling Out Other Conditions

ADHD symptoms often overlap with other disorders, such as anxiety, depression, autism, or learning disabilities. A thorough evaluation ensures that ADHD is correctly diagnosed and not mistaken for another condition.

Step 6: Feedback and Diagnosis

After reviewing the data, the clinician will:

- Provide a diagnosis (if applicable).
- Share a detailed report with findings and recommendations.
- Outline the next steps, including treatment options, school accommodations, and strategies for managing ADHD.

QUESTIONS TO ASK DURING THE ASSESSMENT

1. What tools or methods will be used to evaluate my child?
2. How do you differentiate ADHD from other conditions?
3. Will the assessment include recommendations for school accommodations?
4. How is progress monitored after diagnosis?

COSTS AND INSURANCE COVERAGE

ADHD assessments vary in cost depending on location and type of provider.

- United States: Private evaluations range from $500 to $3,500. Some insurance plans cover part of the cost. Learn more at CHADD.
- Australia: Evaluations typically cost $1,000 to $3,500, with partial Medicare rebates available. Find more details at ADHD Australia.
- United Kingdom: NHS assessments are free, but private evaluations range from £500 to £2,000. More information is available at ADHD UK.

AFTER THE DIAGNOSIS: NEXT STEPS

A diagnosis is the first step in supporting your child's success.

1. Educate Yourself – Resources like ADDitude Magazine provide expert guidance on ADHD management.
2. Explore Treatment Options – Behavioral therapy, medication, and ADHD coaching can improve executive functioning and coping skills.
3. Advocate for School Accommodations – IEPs, 504 Plans, and EHCPs provide necessary learning supports. Learn more at Understood.org.

RECENT DEVELOPMENTS IN ADHD AWARENESS AND SUPPORT

Increased Recognition: Public discussions, advocacy, and social media have reduced stigma and encouraged early diagnosis and intervention.

Advances in Treatment: New non-stimulant medications provide alternative options for those who cannot tolerate stimulants. Digital therapeutic tools (such as EndeavorRx, the first FDA-approved ADHD treatment app) are emerging as effective interventions.

Educational Support Innovations: Schools are implementing sensory-friendly classrooms and teacher training programs to better support students with ADHD.

KEY TAKEAWAYS

1. ADHD assessments involve multiple steps, including interviews, observations, and standardized tests.
2. Costs vary by region—investigate rebates and financial assistance where available.
3. Post-diagnosis support is crucial: explore behavioral, educational, and medical treatment options.
4. Stay informed through trusted organizations and new research to ensure the best support for your child.

An ADHD assessment is an investment in your child's future. By understanding the process and using the available resources, you can confidently advocate for their success and help them reach their full potential.

EXPLAINING ADHD TO YOUR CHILD, STEP-BY-STEP

As a clinical psychologist specializing in ADHD, I've seen many parents wrestle with how to explain this diagnosis to their children. It's a common concern—how do you help your child understand what ADHD is without overwhelming or discouraging them? The way you approach this explanation will differ depending on their age. Over the years, I've found that using gentle metaphors, fostering reassurance, and focusing on strengths helps children of any age better understand their unique minds. In this chapter, I'll share some strategies and examples to help guide your conversation.

TALKING TO CHILDREN AGES 6 TO 8

Children are still learning to name and understand their feelings and behaviors at this young age. Often, they know they have difficulty sitting still or paying attention but don't understand why. It's essential to keep the explanation simple, warm, and reassuring. You might say something like:

"You know how sometimes your body and mind feel really busy, like a playground with lots of swings and slides? That's because your brain works in a special way called ADHD. It can be harder for you to stay still or listen sometimes. It's not your fault; your brain has a lot of fun and bouncy energy! We can work together to find ways to help you feel calm and focus when you need to—just like putting one toy away before you take out another one."

I suggest using fun metaphors that your child can relate to. For example:

- **The Busy Bee:** "Sometimes having ADHD is like being a busy bee, buzzing around a big garden of flowers. You want to see and touch everything! That can make it hard to sit still, but it also means you're curious and full of energy."
- **The Music Band:** "Your mind is like a band playing lots of tunes at once. It can be hard to pick one song to listen to, but having so many tunes means you have lots of fun ideas dancing around."

And always include the positive aspects of ADHD. Let them know:

"Because your brain works differently, you notice things other people miss. You have great ideas and can create fun stories, games, or drawings. You have a brain that's filled with bright, exciting ideas!"

EXPLAINING ADHD TO CHILDREN AGES 9 TO 11

By the time your child approaches the tween years, they have more maturity and may have already sensed that they learn or behave differently than some classmates. They're often ready for a more precise, slightly more detailed explanation. You might say:

"ADHD affects how your brain pays attention, stays organized, and remembers things. It might mean you get distracted easily or feel like you're fast-changing channels on a TV. None of this is your fault. Your brain simply works differently, and many people have ADHD. We can learn ways to help you focus when needed, such as taking short breaks, writing down instructions, or finding calm places to do your homework."

Here are a few metaphors suited to this age group:

- **The TV Channels:** "Your brain is like a TV with many channels. Sometimes, it changes channels before you finish watching one show. That can be tricky, but it also means you're curious about many things."
- **The Hero Headquarters:** "It's like having a bunch of superheroes in your head, all wanting to jump into action at once. Yes, it can get a little noisy, but it means you have many strengths, talents, and interests!"

Emphasize their strengths:

"Because your mind moves quickly, you're great at coming up with creative solutions to problems. You're flexible, can handle surprises,

and are very good at thinking up new games, building unique creations, or telling interesting stories.

EXPLAINING ADHD TO TEENS (12 AND ABOVE)

When your child is in their early teens, they're likely more aware of the world around them—and more self-aware. They might have learned about ADHD from friends, books, or social media. This is a good time to be more direct while still offering encouragement. Consider saying:

"ADHD stands for Attention Deficit Hyperactivity Disorder. It's a term doctors use to describe how some people's brains work differently. You might have noticed you struggle with paying attention in class, following through on tasks, or feeling restless. It's not because you're lazy or not smart—far from it. People with ADHD learn differently and often have incredible creativity and problem-solving skills. Think of your mind as a powerful computer with many open browser tabs. It can be messy, but you can access more interesting ideas than many people do."

Try using more sophisticated metaphors:

- **The Bustling City:** "Your mind is like a city at rush hour—lots of thoughts, ideas, and possibilities all moving simultaneously. We can learn to put up some traffic lights and use maps to navigate that city better."
- **The Canvas of Color:** "It's like your mind is a canvas splashed with many colors. At first, it might seem chaotic, but as you learn strategies, you'll find ways to blend those colors into something amazing that's all your own."

Highlight how ADHD can be a strength:

"Many successful people—artists, inventors, athletes, business leaders—have ADHD. They've learned to use their quick thinking, creativity, and energy to their advantage. You can do the same. With strategies like breaking big tasks into smaller steps, using reminders, or working in a quiet area, you can turn what feels like a challenge into a source of strength."

EMPHASIZING THAT ADHD IS PART OF WHO THEY ARE, NOT ALL THEY ARE

No matter your child's age, they must understand ADHD does not define them. They are not "ADHD kids," they are kids who *have* ADHD. This condition is one part of their identity, but they are also artists, athletes, kind-hearted friends, curious learners, and so much more. Reinforcing this idea helps keep their self-esteem and sense of identity grounded.

FINAL THOUGHTS

Every family is unique, and you know your child best. Adjust your explanations and metaphors to fit their interests and personality. If they love sports, use a sports metaphor; if they're into music, frame ADHD in terms of a band or a playlist. If they adore nature, maybe their mind is a lively forest full of different plants and animals.

Above all, keep the conversation open. Explaining ADHD should not be a one-time event but an ongoing dialogue. You can revisit the topic as your child grows and develops new understanding and coping strategies. By doing so, you're helping your child build a healthy, confident relationship with their brain—a crucial step on their journey to thriving with ADHD.

EXPLORING EFFECTIVE, EVIDENCE-BASED THERAPY OPTIONS FOR CHILDREN WITH ADHD

As a clinical psychologist who has worked with countless families navigating ADHD, one of the most common questions I encounter is, "What therapy options are available, and which ones actually work?" It's natural to feel overwhelmed by the array of treatments you might read or hear about. In this chapter, I'll break down some of the most well-researched, evidence-based interventions and help you understand how they can work together. It's rarely a matter of choosing just one; many children benefit most when different therapies are thoughtfully combined to meet their unique needs.

BEHAVIOR THERAPY

What It Is:

Behavior therapy focuses on teaching children—and often parents—skills to improve behavior, organization, and emotional regulation. This typically involves setting clear rules, routines, and reward systems at home and school.

How It Works:

A therapist trained in behavior therapy might show you how to use a star-chart system where your child earns points for following instructions or completing chores. Over time, these consistent, predictable consequences help your child learn new, more adaptive habits.

+ Pros:

- Evidence-based: Numerous studies show improved behavior, compliance, and parent-child relationships.
- Empowers Parents: You'll learn techniques to use every day at home, increasing consistency and confidence.
- Long-term Skills: Your child develops habits and coping strategies that can last well beyond therapy.

− Cons:

- Requires Consistency: Implementing and maintaining behavior plans can be challenging, especially when life gets busy.
- Gradual Results: It can take time to see significant changes, and some parents become frustrated without immediate improvements.

PARENT TRAINING AND PARENT MANAGEMENT TRAINING (PMT)

What It Is:

Parent training programs, such as Parent Management Training or Parent-Child Interaction Therapy (PCIT), equip you with strategies to respond effectively to challenging behaviors. This support helps create a more stable and supportive home environment.

How It Works:

A psychologist or therapist teaches techniques like giving concise instructions, using positive reinforcement, and applying consistent consequences. Sessions often involve role-playing or live coaching to help you master these tools.

➕ **Pros:**

- Strong Evidence Base: Research consistently supports parent training as a key intervention for ADHD.
- Lasting Impact: By changing how you respond, you help shape your child's behavior and emotional well-being.
- Improves Relationships: As daily conflicts decrease, the parent-child bond typically strengthens.

— Cons:

- Commitment Needed: Parents must be willing to invest time and effort in learning and applying new techniques.
- Emotional Challenges: Shifting long-standing family patterns can be difficult, and you may need to manage your own stress as you implement changes.

MEDICATION (STIMULANTS AND NON-STIMULANTS)

What It Is:

Medications like methylphenidate (Ritalin, Concerta) and amphetamines (Adderall) are considered first-line treatments for ADHD. Non-stimulant options like atomoxetine (Strattera) or certain blood pressure medications may be effective if stimulants are not tolerated.

How It Works:

Stimulants help balance neurotransmitters in the brain, improving attention and reducing impulsivity. Non-stimulants work differently but strive for similar improvements in focus and behavior.

+ Pros:

- Strong Research Support: Numerous studies show medication can significantly reduce core ADHD symptoms.

- Quick Onset: Stimulants often begin to work within hours, providing relatively fast symptom relief.
- Academic and Social Benefits: Improved focus often leads to better performance in school and more positive peer interactions.

— **Cons:**

- Possible Side Effects: Reduced appetite, sleep difficulties, and mood changes can occur.
- No Skill-Building: Medication alone doesn't teach organizational or social skills; it's often best paired with therapy.
- Adjustment Period: Finding the right medication and dosage can involve trial and error.

COGNITIVE BEHAVIORAL THERAPY (CBT) FOR OLDER CHILDREN AND TEENS

What It Is:

CBT helps children understand the connection between their thoughts, feelings, and behaviors. It teaches them strategies to manage impulses, stay organized, and handle challenging emotions—often more appropriate for older kids and teens.

How It Works:

A therapist might guide your child to break tasks into smaller steps, use checklists, and challenge unhelpful thoughts like "I'll never get this right." They learn coping tools they can apply in many areas of life.

+ Pros:

- Skills-Based: Kids learn concrete techniques to improve focus and problem-solving.
- Builds Self-Awareness: Children recognize their patterns and can independently apply new skills.
- Generalizable: Skills apply at school, at home, and social situations.

− Cons:

- Better for Older Kids: Younger children may struggle with the abstract reasoning often required by CBT.
- Requires Practice: CBT strategies need ongoing practice, and results can be gradual rather than immediate.

NEUROFEEDBACK THERAPY

What It Is:

Neurofeedback involves using real-time displays of brain activity—usually measured through EEG—to teach individuals how to regulate their brainwaves. It's a form of biofeedback aimed at improving attention and reducing impulsivity.

How It Works:

Your child might play a computer game that progresses only when their brainwaves show a focused, calm state. Over time, the brain is "trained" to maintain that pattern.

+ Pros:

- Non-Invasive: No medications are involved.
- Potential Skill-Building: Some children report feeling more in control of their concentration after regular sessions.

− Cons:

- Mixed Evidence: While some studies suggest benefits, the scientific consensus isn't as strong as for other treatments.
- Cost and Time: Neurofeedback can be expensive and may require many sessions.
- Varied Results: Not all children benefit equally; research is still exploring the reasons for this.

MINDFULNESS-BASED INTERVENTIONS

What It Is:

Mindfulness training teaches children to pay attention to the present moment, notice their thoughts and feelings without judgment, and develop calm, focused attention.

How It Works:

A therapist might guide short mindfulness exercises—breathing techniques, body scans, or guided imagery—to help the child practice slowing down and tuning in to their inner experience.

+ Pros:

- Promising Evidence: Some research shows mindfulness can improve attention and reduce stress.
- No Side Effects: Natural techniques that support overall well-being.
- Lifelong Skill: Once learned, mindfulness strategies can help in various settings.

− Cons:

- Requires Regular Practice: Results come from consistent effort over time.
- Younger Children's Engagement: Younger kids may need playful adaptations.
- Emerging Field: While encouraging, research is still developing compared to established interventions.

ACADEMIC INTERVENTIONS AND SCHOOL-BASED SUPPORTS

What It Is:

These include 504 Plans or IEPs, specialized tutoring, and classroom accommodations (e.g., extra time on tests, seating arrangements, breaking assignments into smaller steps).

How It Works:

Your child's school team collaborates with you and professionals to create a supportive learning environment tailored to their unique needs.

+ Pros:

- Individualized Support: Tailored to your child's learning style and challenges.
- Boosts Confidence: Academic success can lead to improved self-esteem.
- Legally Supported: In many areas, laws ensure the right to accommodations.

− Cons:

- Advocacy Required: You may need to seek and maintain these supports actively.
- Resource Limitations: School resources vary widely.

ADHD COACHING AND ORGANIZATIONAL SKILLS TRAINING

What It Is:

ADHD coaches or tutors teach organizational skills, time management, and effective study habits, usually best for older children and teens.

How It Works:

A coach might help set up a planner, break projects into smaller steps, or establish a consistent routine. Over time, kids learn to manage responsibilities more independently.

+ Pros:

- Practical Skills: Immediate, tangible tools kids can use every day.
- Builds Independence: Reduces reliance on parents or teachers for organization.
- Complements Other Therapies: Works well alongside medication, behavior therapy, and school support.

− Cons:

- Potential Cost: Often not covered by insurance.
- Motivation Needed: Works best if your child is engaged and willing.

TEACHING SELF-COMPASSION

In addition to these therapies, a crucial piece often goes overlooked: teaching your child to be kind to themselves. Children with ADHD frequently experience frustration, shame, or guilt when they struggle with focus or self-control. They may blame themselves, feeling "lazy" or "not good enough," especially if they've faced criticism or comparisons to peers.

Self-compassion involves understanding that challenges are not their fault, acknowledging that everyone struggles at times, and learning to treat themselves as they would a good friend. Therapies such as CBT and mindfulness can incorporate this element, teaching children to recognize self-critical thoughts and replace them with supportive, understanding ones. Parents can model self-compassion by acknowledging that everyone makes mistakes and celebrating effort as much as outcomes. Over time, children learn that difficulties can be approached with patience and understanding rather than self-judgment.

MY RESEARCH ON MINDFULNESS AND SELF-COMPASSION PROGRAMS

Over the years, I have conducted group-based programs ranging from 6 to 10 weeks, where children and their parents learned skills to enhance mindfulness and self-compassion. Some of the participants had ADHD, and others had Autism Spectrum Disorder (ASD). In these groups, we focused on teaching practical techniques to become more aware of thoughts and emotions, respond more kindly to oneself in moments of frustration, and improve emotional awareness and regulation.

The results were encouraging. Children who participated became kinder to themselves, often replacing harsh self-criticism with more forgiving self-talk. They became more aware of their thoughts and emotions and, importantly, learned strategies to manage them more effectively. While further research is always needed, these findings suggest that incorporating mindfulness and self-compassion into a broader treatment plan can substantially benefit children, helping them build resilience and emotional strength.

COMBINING THERAPIES FOR BETTER RESULTS

Most children with ADHD benefit from a blend of interventions. For example, your child might take a low dose of medication to improve focus while you implement a behavior plan at home. At the same time, a therapist could provide parent training to maintain consistent boundaries, and your child might practice mindfulness exercises to cultivate self-awareness. You could add group sessions that teach self-compassion, or your child works with a coach to improve organizational skills. Meanwhile, school accommodations can ensure academic success.

The process of combining therapies might sound overwhelming; use the steps below to ensure a logical and structured approach:

1. **Begin with one intervention** and assess its impact on your child's attention, impulse control, and/or hyperactivity levels.
2. **Introduce additional therapies one at a time** to allow your child to adjust and to measure their effectiveness individually.
3. **Coordinate with professionals and educators** by sharing goals, progress updates, and challenges to ensure a consistent, collaborative approach.
4. **Monitor and adjust the plan as needed**, recognizing that what works for your child may evolve over time.
5. **Prioritize strategies that support long-term skill-building**, such as executive function coaching or social-emotional learning, alongside immediate symptom management.

By taking a step-by-step, flexible approach, you can create a balanced, personalized intervention plan that supports your child's success in all aspects of life.

A NOTE ON PERSISTENCE AND FLEXIBILITY

ADHD therapy is not a one-time fix. It often requires ongoing adjustments, fine-tuning, and a willingness to try different combinations of treatments. Every child is unique, and what works beautifully for one may need recalibration for another. The key is to remain patient, flexible, and open-minded.

As you explore these options, remember that you're not alone. Therapists, pediatricians, school counselors, coaches, and other professionals can help guide you. Your willingness to advocate, experiment, and stay engaged will help your child develop essential skills, gain confidence, and find their path to success. And through it all, showing them how to be kind to themselves—teaching self-compassion—will give them the emotional tools they need to face challenges with resilience and optimism.

A FUN, FAMILY-FOCUSED MINDFULNESS AND SELF-COMPASSION CURRICULUM
FOR PARENTS AND CHILDREN

Below is a **Family-Focused Mindfulness and Self-Compassion Curriculum** that you can adapt to fit your family's schedule and children's developmental levels. It's laid out over 8 weeks, with each week introducing different practices—everything from guided meditations to paired yoga poses, perspective-taking exercises, and fun sensory activities. Each week has at least **two** suggested activities so you can mix and match what works best for you. Feel free to adjust session lengths and language to suit your child's age and attention span. The key is to create a consistent and playful environment where your family can learn and grow together.

GENERAL TIPS

1. **Session Length**: Aim for about 15 to 30 minutes per session, once, twice, or three times a week. Younger children may benefit from shorter, more frequent activities (5–10 minutes).
2. **Atmosphere**: Find a quiet, comfortable space where everyone can focus. Minimize distractions (e.g., turn off phones and TVs).
3. **Playfulness**: Use child-friendly language and stay flexible. If your child prefers drawing or more movement, incorporate those preferences.
4. **Journaling or Drawing**: After each session, older kids and parents can journal briefly about their experience, and younger kids can draw a picture of how the activity made them feel.
5. **Be Flexible**: If something isn't resonating, try another activity or modify it.

WEEK 1: INTRODUCTION & SETTING INTENTIONS

Activity 1: Family Intention Circle

1. **Gather Together**: Sit in a circle on the floor or around a table.
2. **Explain**: "Mindfulness means paying attention to what's happening here and now, without judging it as good or bad. Self-compassion is being kind to ourselves, especially when we feel upset or make mistakes." Explain that when we practice

Mindfulness and self-compassion, managing our emotions, thoughts, and behaviors becomes easier.
3. **Share Intentions**: Each family member states one intention for the next few weeks. Examples: "I want to learn how to calm down when I'm angry," "I want to learn how to be kinder to myself."
4. **Write or Draw**: If your children enjoy drawing, have them create a simple picture symbolizing their intention. Display these pictures somewhere visible (fridge, corkboard).

Activity 2: Breathing Buddy

1. **Lie Down or Sit Comfortably**: Each person places a small stuffed animal (or pillow) on their belly.
2. **Focus on the Breath**: Inhale for a count of 3, then exhale for a count of 3, watching the stuffed animal rise and fall.
3. **Short Duration**: Aim for 30–60 seconds for younger kids, increasing slowly.
4. **Discussion**: "How did it feel to watch the stuffed animal move with your breath?" Emphasize how focusing on the breath can help us slow down and relax.

WEEK 2: GUIDED MEDITATION & BODY SCAN

Activity 1: Kid-Friendly Guided Meditation (3–5 minutes)

1. **Set Up**: Find a quiet spot and sit on cushions or chairs with feet on the ground.

2. **Script Example** (speak slowly):
   - "Close your eyes or let them rest on a spot on the floor.
   - Take a slow breath in through your nose and gently let it out through your mouth.
   - Imagine you're floating on a soft, fluffy cloud, and the cloud is carrying you safely.
   - Notice how your body feels sitting or lying on this cloud—are your shoulders tense or relaxed?
   - Take a few more calm breaths here…"
3. **Reflect**: Each person shares one word about how they feel, such as "calm," "sleepy," "cozy," etc.

Activity 2: Simple Body Scan (2–3 minutes)

1. **Position**: Lie down or sit upright, whichever is more comfortable.
2. **Step-by-Step**:
   - "Wiggle your toes, then let them rest. Move up to your ankles and notice any tension or relaxation."
   - Continue up through calves, knees, thighs, belly, chest, shoulders, arms, hands, neck, and face.
3. **Finish**: Take one more slow breath.
4. **Discussion**: "Where did you feel tense? Do you feel more relaxed now?"

WEEK 3: MINDFUL MOVEMENT & GENTLE YOGA

Activity 1: Mindful Movement – "Slow Motion"

1. **Pick a Simple Action**: Walking across the room, picking up toys, or gently stretching your arms.
2. **Move Very Slowly**: Encourage everyone to move like turtles, paying attention to each muscle as it moves.
3. **Observation**: "What do you notice when we move slowly? How does it feel in your body?"

Activity 2: Paired Yoga Poses

1. **Seated Back-to-Back Breathing**
    - Sit back-to-back on the floor, legs crossed.
    - Inhale and exhale together, noticing the gentle pressure of each other's backs.
    - Feel how you can support each other just by being there.
2. **Partner Tree Pose**
    - Stand side by side. Each lifts the foot furthest from the other person, placing the food on the inner calf or thigh. This allows you to lean on each other for support.
    - Hold hands or shoulders for balance. Try a few breaths, then switch sides.

WEEK 4: NATURE WALK & SENSORY AWARENESS

Activity 1: Family Nature Walk (15–30 minutes)

1. **Prepare**: Let everyone know you'll be paying attention to your surroundings in a mindful way.
2. **Five Senses Check-Ins**:
     - **Sight**: "Find something you've never noticed before."
     - **Sound**: "Pause. Close your eyes for 10 seconds and listen."
     - **Touch**: "Touch a leaf or tree bark—notice how it feels."
     - **Smell**: "Do you smell anything (grass, flowers, fresh air)?"
     - **Taste** (only if appropriate, like a safe snack or water).
3. **Reflection**: Share one surprising thing you noticed.

Activity 2: Nature Gratitude Circle

1. **Form a Circle**: Stand together in a calm spot outdoors.
2. **Each Person Shares**: One thing in nature they're grateful for—sunshine, birds, a breeze.
3. **Link to Self-Compassion**: Remind each other that, like nature, we go through changes, too. Being gentle with ourselves is part of this process.

WEEK 5: PERSPECTIVE-TAKING & EMPATHY

Activity 1: Role-Play "Through Another's Eyes"

1. **Pick a Scenario**: Something relatable (e.g., a sibling took your toy, or a friend was teasing you at school).
2. **Act It Out**: Child and parent take turns playing each role—victim and "perpetrator."
3. **Discussion**: "How did it feel to be in the other person's shoes? Does this change how you react next time?"

Activity 2: "I Notice, I Feel, I Need" Practice

1. **Explain the Formula**:
    - "I Notice…" (the situation: "We keep arguing when it's time to do homework.")
    - "I Feel…" (the emotion: "I feel stressed or annoyed.")
    - "I Need…" (a request or wish: "I need us to take a 5-minute break before starting homework.")
2. **Family Sharing**: Go around and let each member use this format for a real or hypothetical problem.
3. **Benefits**: Reduces blaming and fosters clearer communication.

WEEK 6: "BE YOUR OWN CHEERLEADER"

Activity 1: Creating Personal Mantras

1. **Explain**: "A mantra is like a positive cheer we say to ourselves."
2. **Examples**:
   - "I'm doing my best, and that's enough."
   - "I can handle this."
   - "I'm learning every day."
3. **Family Creation**: Each person writes or draws their mantra. Display them in a spot where they'll be seen daily (e.g., bedroom mirror).

Activity 2: Mirror Work (Optional but Powerful)

1. **Stand in Front of a Mirror**: Parent and child can do this together or separately.
2. **Say Your Mantra**: Out loud, while looking at yourself.
3. **Offer Self-Praise**: "I'm proud of how I tried something new."
4. **Reflection**: Acknowledge that it may feel awkward but emphasize the importance of learning to be kind to oneself.

WEEK 7: SENSORY EXPLORATION & EMOTIONAL EXPRESSION

Activity 1: Sensory Stations

1. **Set Up**: Create mini stations around a room or table, each focusing on a different sense or texture. Examples:
    - **Texture Tray**: Fill a tray with rice, sand, or beans for children to run their fingers through.
    - **Sound Corner**: Small instruments (bells, shakers).
    - **Aromatherapy Spot**: Cotton balls with soothing scents (lavender, citrus).
2. **Rotate Stations**: Spend 1–2 minutes at each station, noticing how the senses react.
3. **Discussion**: "Which station made you feel calm or excited?"

Activity 2: Emotional Color Splash

1. **Paper & Paint/Crayons**: Each person chooses a color that represents their current emotion.
2. **Draw or Paint Freely**: Encourage various strokes—big, small, swirling—whatever expresses that emotion.
3. **Share**: "What does this color or shape mean to you? Did your emotion change while you were creating?"

WEEK 8: CELEBRATION & INTEGRATION

Activity 1: Family "Show & Tell"

1. **Recap**: Each family member shares their favorite practice from the past seven weeks (e.g., a specific yoga pose, a mantra, mindful eating).
2. **Demonstration**: If it's something physical like yoga, demonstrate briefly. If it's a mantra, say it together.

Activity 2: Future Mindfulness Plan

1. **Collaborate**: Discuss which practices you want to continue.
2. **Create a Simple Schedule**:
   - Mondays: 2-minute Breathing Buddy
   - Wednesdays: Mindful Movement or quick Nature Walk
   - Fridays: "I Notice, I Feel, I Need" check-in
   - Weekends: Sensory play or yoga together
3. **Affirm Each Other**: Remind each other that Mindfulness and self-compassion are lifelong skills. Small, steady practice is key.

KEEPING THE JOURNEY GOING

Now that you have the tools to build confidence, connection, and consistency in your child's life, it's time to share what you've learned and help others on the same path.

By leaving your honest opinion of this book on Amazon, you'll guide other parents who are searching for answers—just like you once were. Your review could be the signpost that leads them to the support, understanding, and strategies they need to thrive.

Parenting a child with ADHD isn't a solo journey. We learn from each other, we grow together, and we keep this knowledge alive by passing it forward.

Thank you for being part of this mission. Every review, every shared experience, helps another family take a step towards less stress and more connection.

https://www.amazon.com/review/create-review/?asin=B0DY9KG561

With gratitude,

- Dr. Victoria Barclay-Timmis

AUTHOR BIOGRAPHY

Dr. Victoria Barclay-Timmis is a compassionate clinical psychologist, university lecturer, researcher, and mother. Originally from the UK, she transitioned from a career in advertising and marketing to psychology after moving to Australia in 2003. Her diverse experiences, including travel and parenthood, have deepened her appreciation for cultural diversity and her commitment to helping others. In 2019, she completed a PhD focusing on self-compassion, mindfulness, resilience, and well-being for children and parents. Dr. Barclay-Timmis is also accredited in Emotional Freedom Techniques (EFT) and is involved in clinical research to explore its benefits. As co-director of Lavender House Wellness Collective, she is dedicated to empowering clients to lead fulfilling lives and supports early-career psychologists in reaching their potential.

This is the first book authored by Dr. Victoria Barclay-Timmis. Inspiration came from the lived experience of parenting a child with ADHD, and a desire to help as many families as possible raise confident, connected children.

BIBLIOGRAPHY AND REFERENCE LIST

PEER-REVIEWED JOURNAL ARTICLES

Barclay-Timmis, V. S., Burton, L. J., & Beccaria, G. (2023). The development and psychometric evaluation of two new scales of self-compassion for preadolescents. *Measurement Instruments for the Social Sciences, 5*(1), Article e11199. https://doi.org/10.5964/miss.11199

Bögels, S. M., Hoogstad, B., van Dun, L., de Schutter, S., & Restifo, K. (2011). The effectiveness of mindfulness training for children with ADHD and mindful parenting for their parents. *Journal of Child and Family Studies, 20*(2), 1–12. https://pmc.ncbi.nlm.nih.gov/articles/PMC3267931/

Cortese, S., Kelly, C., Chabernaud, C., Proal, E., Di Martino, A., Milham, M. P., & Castellanos, F. X. (2014). Understanding attention deficit disorder: A neuroscience perspective. *Nature Reviews Neuroscience, 15*(10), 632–643. https://pmc.ncbi.nlm.nih.gov/articles/PMC4009719/

Daley, D., & Birchwood, J. (2010). ADHD and academic attainment: What have we learned? *Current Psychiatry Reports, 12*(5), 357–363. https://doi.org/10.1007/s11920-010-0133-5

Graziano, P. A., & Garcia, A. (2016). ADHD and children's emotion regulation: Research and clinical implications. *Clinical Child and Family Psychology Review, 19*(3), 219–242. https://doi.org/10.1007/s10567-016-0212-6

Hinshaw, S. P. (2018). Attention deficit hyperactivity disorder (ADHD), developmental trajectories, and adult outcomes: An integrative approach. *Psychological Bulletin, 144*(6), 634–659. https://doi.org/10.1037/bul0000153

Kolko, D. J., Campo, J. V., Kelleher, K., & Cheng, Y. (2015). Collaborative care for children with ADHD symptoms: A randomized clinical trial. *JAMA Pediatrics, 169*(2), 1–9. https://pubmed.ncbi.nlm.nih.gov/25802346/

Pelham, W. E., Fabiano, G. A., & Massetti, G. M. (2005). Evidence-based assessment of attention deficit hyperactivity disorder in children and adolescents. *Journal of Clinical Child and Adolescent Psychology, 34*(3), 449–476. https://doi.org/10.1207/s15374424jccp3403_5

Shaw, P., Stringaris, A., Nigg, J., & Leibenluft, E. (2014). Emotion dysregulation in attention deficit hyperactivity disorder. *American Journal of Psychiatry, 171*(3), 276–293. https://doi.org/10.1176/appi.ajp.2013.13070966

Sonuga-Barke, E. J. S., Daley, D., Thompson, M., Laver-Bradbury, C., & Weeks, A. (2001). Parent-based therapies for ADHD: A review of evidence and recommendations. *Clinical Psychology Review, 21*(4), 449–476. https://doi.org/10.1016/S0272-7358(99)00061-5

Van der Oord, S., Prins, P. J. M., Oosterlaan, J., & Emmelkamp, P. M. G. (2008). Efficacy of mindfulness training for children with ADHD and their parents. *Journal of Child Psychology and Psychiatry, 49*(10), 982–990. https://doi.org/10.1111/j.1469-7610.2008.01924.x

Young, S., Amarasinghe, J. M., & Mills, C. J. (2020). Cognitive behavioral therapy (CBT) for children with ADHD: A meta-analytic review. *Clinical Child Psychology and Psychiatry, 25*(3), 523–541. https://adhdinchildrensupport.com/cbt-cognitive-behavioural-therapy-for-children-with-adhd/

BOOKS

Barkley, R. A. (2013). *Taking charge of ADHD: The complete, authoritative guide for parents* (3rd ed.). Guilford Press.

Brown, T. E. (2014). *Smart but stuck: Emotions in teens and adults with ADHD.* Jossey-Bass.

Dawson, P., & Guare, R. (2018). *Smart but scattered: The revolutionary "executive skills" approach to helping kids reach their potential.* Guilford Press.

Hallowell, E. M., & Ratey, J. J. (2021). *ADHD 2.0: New science and essential strategies for thriving with distraction—From childhood through adulthood.* Ballantine Books.

Hinshaw, S. P. (2018). *Another kind of madness: A journey through the stigma and hope of mental illness.* St. Martin's Press.

Maté, G. (2011). *Scattered minds: The origins and healing of attention deficit disorder.* Random House Canada.

Shaywitz, S. (2020). *Overcoming dyslexia: Second edition, completely revised and updated.* Knopf.

Tuckman, A. (2012). *More attention, less deficit: Success strategies for adults with ADHD.* Specialty Press.

WEBSITES AND ONLINE RESOURCES

ADDitude Magazine. (n.d.). Retrieved from https://www.additudemag.com

ADHD Foundation. (n.d.). Retrieved from https://www.adhdfoundation.org.uk

American Psychiatric Association. (2013). *Diagnostic and statistical manual of mental disorders* (5th ed.). https://doi.org/10.1176/appi.books.9780890425596

International Obsessive Compulsive Disorder Foundation. (n.d.). OCD and ADHD Dual Diagnosis Misdiagnosis and the Cognitive 'Cost' of Obsessions. Retrieved from https://iocdf.org/expert-opinions/expert-opinion-ocd-and-adhd-dual-diagnosis-misdiagnosis-and-the-cognitive-cost-of-obsessions/

Mayo Clinic. (n.d.). Attention-deficit/hyperactivity disorder (ADHD) in children. Retrieved from https://www.mayoclinic.org/diseases-conditions/adhd/symptoms-causes/syc-20350889

National Institute of Mental Health. (n.d.). Attention-deficit/hyperactivity disorder (ADHD): Symptoms and diagnosis. Retrieved from https://www.nimh.nih.gov

www.ingramcontent.com/pod-product-compliance
Lightning Source LLC
Chambersburg PA
CBHW071239070526
44583CB00017B/2250